That Which is Seen and That Whic[h]

Together with

What is Government?

and

Petition of the Candlemakers.

Frédéric Bastiat

Member of The Institute of France

Introduced and edited by Gary Furnell

Foreword by Peter Fenwick

Connor Court Publishing

Published in 2024 by Connor Court Publishing Pty Ltd.

Connor Court Publishing Pty Ltd
PO Box 7257
Redland Bay QLD 4165
sales@connorcourt.com
www.connorcourt.com
Phone 0497-900-685

Printed and bound in Australia.

ISBN: 9781922815927

Front cover design: Tim Jones.

The Philosophical Notes
No.2

Previous Volume

The Evolution of Evolution by St. George Jackson Mivart

CONTENTS

6

FOREWORD

Nassim Taleb once opined that what your professor said in his lecture today was probably wrong, but if you were reading something written ten or twenty or fifty or a hundred years ago, that was still in print, it was probably true. It had stood the test of time.

Frédéric Bastiat's work is like that. He wrote in the 1840s. His work is still in print. It is much quoted. It has influenced the Austrian School of economics – thinkers like Mises, Hayek and Rothbard. Today, there is a Bastiat Society based in Great Barrington in Massachusetts USA with chapters all over the world.

The essence of Bastiat's thought is that good economic policy requires that you consider both the immediate and the long-term consequences, and that you consider the effect not just on one group but on all groups. One hundred years after Bastiat, Henry Hazlitt expanded on these ideas in his book *Economics in One Lesson.* It too is still in print.

Bastiat wrote for everyman. His writing is clear and easy to understand. He was the first economic journalist. One of the best ever. He was frequently witty too, often using *reductio ad absurdum* to make his case. In *A Negative Railway* he discussed a proposed railway from Paris to Madrid. It had been suggested that it would be economically advantageous to have a forced break at Bordeaux, thereby creating work for the bargemen, porters, commissionaires, hotelkeepers and warehousemen of that city. Bastiat responded that it should also break at Angouleme, Poitiers, Tours, Orleans – in fact, that it should break at all intermediate points, thus creating work for the citizens of all these towns! On free trade, in his *Petition on Behalf of the Candlemakers,* he hoisted the protectionists on their own petard. He called for the Deputies to force Parisians to shutter their windows to protect the candlemakers from the unfair competition from the sun.

In *The Law,* he exposed *moral* and *economic* deficiencies. He told how governments, instead of protecting the lives, liberties, and property of their citizens, engage in *legal plunder.* They rob some people of legitimately earned wealth in order to provide the chosen and themselves with unearned benefits. And in *The State,* he explained the consequence: "The state is the great fictitious entity by which everyone seeks to live at the expense of everyone else".

In this edition of *That Which is Seen and That Which is Not Seen,* Gary Furnell expertly makes the text easily understood by the modern reader without sacrificing the richness of Bastiat's style nor his urgency and passion for a free society.

This book will change how you view your world. Now, you will apply *foresight* as you examine the consequences of economic policies. Learning from Bastiat's timeless examples, you will be able to identify the errors in contemporary proposals.

In resurrecting Frédéric Bastiat, Gary Furnell has provided you with the wherewithal to apply common sense to economics and a starting point for a lifetime of intellectual adventure.

Peter Fenwick

August 2023

The Philosophical Notes edition of
That Which is Seen and
That Which is Not Seen

That Which is Seen and That Which is Not Seen is witty and enlightening. Those aren't the usual descriptors of an economics book. But Bastiat knew his insights were more likely to be considered and embraced if they were delivered in a persuasively light tone. He also knew that arcane jargon and prolixity were the common obfuscations of politicians and their treasury officials, so plain speech and easily understood examples would aid his readers' understanding. In economics, as in philosophy, clarity is courtesy.

The result is an enduring work combining brevity, levity and depth.

Bastiat's wit is mocking but never nasty. He uses it to ridicule errors or to elucidate ideas rather than to denigrate opponents. He must have been sorely aggravated by some of the stupidities he saw in the French government, but he seems a polite, even-tempered writer.

His sympathies were with the common man who was so often scorned and exploited. He uses *James Goodman* as a type of this longsuffering but sensible yeoman in several of his examples. In Bastiat's words, it was best to *Trust the people, not the legislators*.

Nearly one hundred years after Bastiat, another French champion of liberty and common dignity, Jacques Maritain, in his book *Man and the State*, wrote that trusting the people was the basis of democracy. This doesn't mean the human propensity to greed, laziness or any other vice is discounted. Rather, it means acknowledging that the majority of people possess solid common sense.

Alas! Bastiat would exclaim, governments don't trust the people, instead presuming to harangue them while interfering with their businesses, embedded values and everyday affairs.

The details of Bastiat's life can be given briefly because information about him is easily found on various websites. Claude-Frédéric Bastiat (1801-1850) was born near Bayonne in south-western France. Orphaned while a young boy, he was brought up by his aunt and his grandfather, a wealthy farmer. At the age of seventeen, Frederic went to work for his uncle, a merchant. This experience was crucial because Bastiat learned the realities of practical business and also saw how government edicts impacted businesses.

He inherited a sizeable estate and thereby became, while still a young man, independent. He studied and developed useful public service capabilities. He became a Justice of the Peace and a member of the local legislature. He was later elected to the National Assembly. He also wrote, publishing books and articles on economics and politics in the 1840s.

Unfortunately, Bastiat contracted tuberculosis. In 1850, he was sent by his doctor to the warmer, drier climate of Italy but died aged 49 in Rome.

This translation of *That Which is Seen and That Which is Unseen* was published in 1874. I've made minor, but I hope helpful amendments to this translation, substituting commonly used words for little known words or those whose meaning has changed. Footnotes have been added to provide context. Some longer paragraphs have been broken into two shorter paragraphs to help understanding. The aim is to introduce Bastiat to the general reader.

One of the benefits of reading books or translations from a previous age is the delight found in the different styles. I've left as much as possible of the rich, older language because it's a valuable part of the reading experience. Not one of Bastiat's principle points is antiquated. The book is as relevant now as it was to France in the mid-nineteenth century. Today, the unseen consequences of policies are overlooked because we're not trained to look for—or foresee—the consequences; also, in some circumstances, time only slowly reveals the results.

Bastiat wants to bring both seen and unseen aspects of economic policies to our view and to fix that manner of looking in our minds. He uses the story of the broken window as an illustrative preamble to the next chapters. He explains that damaged assets are not an obvious occasion for profitable activity when every aspect, including those overlooked, is considered. It's a point he repeats, applied to different settings.

Maintaining the size of the military to benefit the national economy is a still popular idea. We're told that enlarging the forces or creating new defence bases is good for the economy. Bastiat disentangles the truth from the error. Military spending concentrates rather than disperses wealth; it takes money out of the hands of many diversely-located tax-payers and puts it into the bank accounts of bureaucrats, a few businesses in a few regions and defence force personnel who—when not defending the country—aren't as productively employed as any worker in any privately-owned business. Of course, we need a strong, well-trained military, but not as an employment or regional development scheme.

His insights into military spending apply to tax spending generally when it's spent to generate jobs and business activity. Yes, someone benefits *here*, but someone loses *there*.

Support for arts follows the same pattern. It's refreshing to note Bastiat affirming the elevated morals, the education in aesthetics and the refined sensibilities shining from the arts of his day. These aren't the salient qualities everywhere evident in contemporary arts. Kitschy baubles, abrasive and ridiculous posturing, works expressing lame politically correct attitudes or nihilistic misanthropy are celebrated. And all at the taxpayer's expense. Bastiat asks, if the arts are as vibrantly fruitful as their supporters proclaim, why are they reliant on tradespeople's taxes?

Asking this question invites accusations of Philistinism and an anti-arts agenda as if tax-payer support was the only possible support. Bastiat wants the arts to flourish, and they do flourish. Theatres and writers, painters and musicians can be successful without government funds. For example, the wide varieties of popular music have been amazingly successful—and profitable—for many decades without subsidies. Creative people love their art and the best of them don't need grants from bureaucrats to develop, showcase and make a living from their talent. It may not be easy, but neither is being a mortician, a surgeon or a welder.

Bastiat alludes in this book to corruption as a serious injustice inflicted on the tax-payer. Mostly, he uses economic logic to expose common fallacies. But he knows corruption is another factor distorting decision-making and limiting diversified gain. Cronyism and bribery are always lurking around large public works and are unwelcome greasers of the trade-restrictive privileges granted to particular industries or businesses. Wealth directed to one entity is wealth unjustly directed away from another.

The socialist dream of a centrally-organised, bureaucratically-administered economy is given a hammering. Since Bastiat's time, this idea has been tried repeatedly and everywhere it's been a disaster: freedom, privacy and innovation have been curtailed, while torment, dependence and scarcity have spiralled beyond imaginable bounds. He foresaw the economic disaster, but few foresaw the extent of the cruelty. Dostoyevsky foresaw it. Hundreds of millions of people lived it—and tens of millions died from it.

Trade restrictions are like a broken window. Any damage, in the form of restrictions, to businesses or industry cannot be justified by the claim that jobs are somehow protected or created. Always, other jobs are lost. In addition, restrictions lessen competition. Competition is always good for the consumer, lowering prices and fostering innovation. Ironically, restrictions are an injustice perpetrated by the government—which is supposed to maintain law and order. *Petition of the Candle-makers* has been included because it makes these points with engaging satire.

Technological change was a challenge to people in nineteenth-century Europe just as it is to us. It's encouraging to learn about the widespread benefits of efficient technology. Broadly speaking, entrepreneurs and innovators, far from gaining advantages only for themselves, scatter their enriching gifts to *many* people.

Governments want to spread prosperity but choose the wrong ways to achieve this worthy goal. Interference in the banking system, especially by helping insolvent or negligent people to access credit, invites calamity. The first two decades of this century, in the United States in particular, have demonstrated that Bastiat was right and market manipulators were badly wrong. Someone always pays the bill: usually the powerless people who had no part in formulating the foolish policy.

People who work for themselves are dependably more motivated than public servants. Government officials rarely work more cost-effectively than people in private enterprise. Too often, the taxes of diligent people are taken to pay officials who then *frustrate* the work of the tax-payers. This problem hasn't gone away; perhaps it never will because some government is necessary, but the debilitation can be minimised.

Minimising taxes is a step in the right direction. Taxes spent by governments don't spread wealth equitably, and they don't create new jobs or industries—they merely displace jobs and industries. Taxes don't add to a nation's economy. For this reason, ancient kings, wiser than our treasury advisors, taxed resident *foreigners* before they taxed citizens. This form of taxation brought money into the realm.

Individuals who are thrifty and save their money will find their good habits ratified. Their ongoing beneficence is brought to our view. Money saved isn't money lost; it circulates widely in overlooked ways. When governments try to stimulate an economy by spending (and often enough spending with borrowed money), it's never anywhere near as effective as stimulating an economy through long-term savings and shrewd investing. Few politicians or treasury officials seem to understand this reality.

Wages fixed or jobs secured by politicians or their bureaucrats are another distortion imposed on a nation. This form of interference locks in unproductive practices and delays fruitful changes. A good economy is a dynamic economy. Industries come and go as social conditions and technologies change, but governments try to forestall this and protect wages or favoured jobs. A loss of wealth for the whole country is the inevitable result. Some people have coddled jobs, but other people pay the cost for the moribund contrivance as damaging inefficiencies are prolonged.

Small government focussed on ensuring security and liberty is the best government. The overwhelming majority of people can be relied upon to look after themselves and their family—graciously helping their friends and community when needed—without the expensive, freedom-trampling burden of bullying government. When people expect much from the government they must expect high taxes to pay for the largesse. A great deal of government instability results when much is expected—or promised—but with low taxation; it's an impossible situation. Governments may borrow or print money to make up the difference, but this only postpones the inevitable instability.

Individuals need to be responsible and prudent. This rugged sturdiness may appear frightening in our welfare state, but that's only because we're constantly conditioned in subtle ways to see ourselves as ever-vulnerable and insufficiently capable.

Frédéric Bastiat was wary of abstractions such as *France* (as if it was a real person with aims, emotions and wants) or concepts like *association* or *fraternity* when used to stir the intemperate passions of idealistic radicals. He preferred effective existing co-operatives and mutual-aid societies. They embodied real association and worthy fraternity, with participation freely chosen.

He was also wary of human pretence. Not one of us is perfect; neither can we achieve anything perfect. Virtues, especially honesty and justice, are the best basis for any human activity. The world is too complex to understand in its entirety and therefore our boldest all-encompassing political dreams are dangerous. Bastiat quotes from Chateaubriand to this effect. It's wiser to respect our nature and our limits, work with the world and its incredible resources, honour providence—and each other—with modesty. This may seem a humble goal but, paradoxically, it exalts humanity.

Gary Furnell

Introduction

In the department of economy, an act, a habit, an institution, a law, gives birth not only to an effect, but to a series of effects. Of these effects, the first only is immediate; it manifests itself simultaneously with its cause—*it is seen*. The others unfold in succession—*they are not seen*. It would be better for us if they are *foreseen*. Between a good and a bad economist this constitutes the whole difference—one takes account of the *visible* effect; the other takes account both the effects which are *seen* and those which it is necessary to *foresee*. Now this difference is enormous, for it almost always happens that when the immediate consequence is favourable, the ultimate consequences are fatal, and the converse applies too. Hence it follows that the bad economist pursues a small present good, which will be followed by a great evil to come, while the true economist pursues a great good to come, at the risk of a small present evil.

In fact, it is the same in the science of health, arts, and in that of morals. If often happens, that the sweeter the first fruit of a habit is the more bitter are the consequences. Take, for example, debauchery, idleness, recklessness. When, therefore, a man absorbed in the effect which *is seen* has not yet learned to discern those which are *not seen*, he gives way to fatal habits not only by inclination, but by calculation.

This explains the fatally grievous condition of mankind. Ignorance surrounds its cradle: then its actions are determined by their first consequences, the only ones which, in its first stage, it can see. It is only in the long run that it learns to take account of the others. It has to learn this lesson from two very different masters: experience and foresight. Experience teaches effectually, but brutally. It makes us acquainted with all the effects of an action by causing us to feel them; and we cannot fail to learn that fire burns if we have burned ourselves. Instead of this rough teacher, I should like, if possible, to substitute a gentler one: foresight. For this purpose I shall examine the consequences of certain economic phenomena by placing in opposition to each other effects *which are seen* and those *which are not seen.*

1. The Broken Window

Have you ever witnessed the anger of the good shopkeeper, James Goodman, when his careless son happened to break a pane of glass? If you have been present at such a scene you will most assuredly bear witness to the fact that every one of the spectators, were there even thirty of them, by common consent apparently, offered the unfortunate owner this invariable consolation, "It is an ill wind that blows nobody good. Everybody must live, and what would become of the glaziers if panes of glass were never broken?"

Now, this form of condolence contains an entire theory which it will be well to explain in this simple case, seeing that it is precisely the same as that which, unhappily, regulates the greater part of our economic institutions.

Suppose it cost six *francs*[1] to repair the damage, and you say that the accident brings six *francs* to the glazier's trade—that it encourages that trade to the amount of six *francs*—I grant it; I have not a word to say against it; you reason justly. The glazier comes, performs his task, receives his six *francs*, rubs his hands, and, in his heart, blesses the careless child. All this is *that which is seen*.

But if, on the other hand, you come to the conclusion, as is too often the case, that it is a good thing to break windows, that it causes money to circulate and that the encouragement of industry

---

1   A note on French currency of the time: 5 *centimes* made 1 *sous*; 20 *sous* in a *franc*.

in general will be the result of it, you will oblige me to call out, "Stop there! Your theory is confined to *that which is seen*; it takes no account of *that which is not seen*."

It is not seen that because our shopkeeper has spent six *francs* upon one thing, he cannot spend them upon another. It is not seen that if he had not had a window to replace, he would, perhaps, have replaced his old shoes or added another book to his library. In short, he would have employed his six *francs* in some way which the broken pane has prevented.

Let us take a view of industry in general, as affected by this circumstance. The window being broken, the glazier's trade is encouraged to the amount of six *francs*: this is that which is seen.

If the window had not been broken, the shoemaker's trade (or some other) would have been encouraged to the amount of six *francs*: this is that which is not seen.

And if that which is not seen is taken into consideration, because it is a negative fact, as well as that which is seen, because it is a positive fact, it will be understood that neither industry in general, nor the sum total of national labour, is affected, whether windows are broken or not.

Now let us consider James Goodman himself. In the former supposition, that of the window being broken, he spends six *francs* and has neither more nor less than he had before: the enjoyment of a window.

In the second, where we suppose the window not to have been broken, he would have spent six *francs* in shoes and would have had at the same time enjoyed a new pair of shoes *and* a window.

Now, as James Goodman forms a part of society, we must come to the conclusion that, taking it altogether, and making an estimate of its enjoyments and its labours, society has lost the value of the broken window.

Thus we arrive at this unexpected conclusion: "Society loses the value of things which are uselessly destroyed." And we must affirm a maxim which will make the hair of protectionists stand on end: To break, to spoil, to waste, is not to encourage national labour; or, more briefly, "destruction is not profit."

What will you say, Moniteur Industriel[2]? What will you say, disciples of good Monsieur Chamans[3], who has calculated with so much precision how much trade would gain by the burning of Paris, from the number of houses it would be necessary to rebuild?

I am sorry to disturb these ingenious calculations, as far as their spirit has been introduced into our legislation; but I beg him to begin them again, by taking into the account that which is not seen and placing it alongside of that which is seen.

The reader must take care to remember that there are not two persons only, but three concerned in the little scene which I have submitted to his attention. One of them, James Goodman, represents the consumer, reduced by an act of destruction to one enjoyment instead of two. Another, under the title of the glazier, shows us the producer whose trade is encouraged by the accident. The third is the shoemaker (or some other tradesman) whose labour suffers proportionally from the accident.

---

2   *Le Moniteur Industriel* was a French protectionist journal.

3   Auguste Louis Philippe de Saint-Chamans (1777-1860) was a French politician and economist who posited that the great fire of London, due to the spending on re-building, constituted a net economic gain.

It is this third person who is always kept in the shade, and who, embodying that which is not seen is a necessary element of the problem. It is he who shows us how absurd it is to think we see a profit in an act of destruction. It is he who will soon teach us that it is also absurd to see a profit in trade restrictions which are, after all, nothing else than a partial destruction. Therefore, if you will only go to the root of all the arguments which are adduced in its favour, all you will find will be the paraphrase of this silly saying: What would become of the glaziers, if nobody ever broke windows?

2. The Disbanding of Troops

It is the same with a country as it is with a man. If it wishes to give itself some gratification, it naturally considers whether the gratification is worth what it costs. To a nation, security is the greatest of advantages. If in order to obtain it, it is necessary to have an army of a hundred thousand men, I have nothing to say against it. It is an enjoyment bought by a sacrifice. Let me not be misunderstood upon the extent of my position.

Now, a member of the assembly proposes to disband a hundred thousand men, for the sake of relieving the tax-payers of a hundred millions.

If we confine ourselves to this answer: "The hundred millions of men, and these hundred millions of money, are indispensable to the national security: it is a sacrifice but without this sacrifice France would be torn by factions or invaded by some foreign power," I have nothing to object to this argument, which may be true or false in fact, but which theoretically contains nothing which confounds good economic sense.

The error begins when the sacrifice itself is said to be an advantage because it profits somebody.

Now I am very much mistaken if, the moment the author of the proposal has taken his seat, some orator will rise to say,

"Disband a hundred thousand men! Do you know what

you are saying? What will become of them? Where will they get a living? Don't you know that work is scarce everywhere? That every field is over-stocked? Would you turn them out of doors to increase competition, lowering the rate of wages? Just now, when it is a hard matter to live at all, it would be a pretty thing if the State must find bread for a hundred thousand individuals? Consider, besides, that the army consumes wine, arms, clothing—that it promotes the activity of manufactures in garrison towns—that it is, in short, the godsend of innumerable suppliers. Why, any one must tremble at the bare idea of doing away with this immense industrial movement."

This discourse, it is evident, concludes by voting the maintenance of a hundred thousand soldiers, for reasons drawn from the necessity of military service and from economic considerations. It is the economic considerations only that I want to refute.

A hundred thousand men, costing the tax-payers a hundred millions of money, live and bring to the suppliers as much as a hundred millions can supply. This is that which is seen.

But a hundred million taken from the pockets of the tax-payers ceases to maintain these tax-payers and their suppliers, as far as a hundred millions reach. This is that which is not seen. Now make your calculations. Cast up and tell me what profit there is for the masses?

I will tell you where the *loss* lies; and to simplify it, instead of speaking of a hundred thousand men and a hundred millions of money it shall be of one man and a thousand *francs*.

We will suppose that we are in the village of A. The recruiting sergeants go their round, and take off a man. The tax-gatherers go their round, and take off a thousand *francs*. The man and the sum of money are taken to Metz[4], and the money is destined to support the soldier for a year without doing anything. If you consider Metz only you are quite right; the measure is a very advantageous one. But if you look towards the village of A., you will judge very differently; for unless you are very blind indeed you will see that that village has lost a worker, and the thousand *francs* wages which he would have been paid for his labour as well as the activity which, by the expenditure of those thousand *francs*, it would spread around it.

At first sight, there would seem to be some compensation. What took place at the village, now takes place at Metz, that is all. But the loss is to be estimated in this way: at the village a man dug and worked; he was a worker. At Metz he turns to the right and to the left about; he is a soldier. The money and the circulation are the same in both cases; but in the one there were three hundred days of productive labour, in the other there are three hundred days of unproductive labour. Supposing, of course, that a part of the army is not required for public safety.

Now, suppose the disbanding to take place. You tell me there will be a surplus of a hundred thousand workers, that competition will be stimulated, and it will reduce the rate of wages. This is what you see.

But what you do not see is this. You do not see that to dismiss a hundred thousand soldiers is not to do away with a hundred million *francs*, but to return it to the tax-payers. You do not see that to throw a hundred thousand workers on the labour market is to throw into it, at the same moment, the hundred million *francs* needed to

---

4   Metz, a French town, long associated with garrisoned troops.

pay for their labour. Consequently, the same act which increases the labour supply increases also the demand for labour; from which it follows, that your fear of a reduction of wages is unfounded. You do not see that, before the disbanding as well as after it, there are in the country a hundred millions *francs* corresponding with the hundred thousand men. That the whole difference consists in this: before the disbanding, the country gave the hundred million *francs* to the hundred thousand men for doing nothing; and that after it, it pays them the same sum for working. You do not see, in short, that when a tax-payer gives his money either to a soldier in exchange for nothing, or to a worker in exchange for something, all the ultimate consequences of the circulation of this money are the same in the two cases? The difference is that in the second case the tax-payer receives *something*, in the former he receives *nothing*. The result is a dead loss to the nation.

The sophism which I am here combating will not stand the test of progression, which is the touchstone of principles. If, when every compensation is made and all interests satisfied, there is a national profit in increasing the army, why not enrol under its banners the entire male population of the country?

3. Taxes

Have you never chanced to hear it said: "There is no better investment than taxes. Only see what a number of families it maintains, and consider how it stimulates industry: it is an inexhaustible stream, it is life itself."

In order to combat this doctrine, I must refer to my preceding refutation. Political economy knew well enough that its arguments were not so amusing that it could be said of them, *repetition please!* It has, therefore, turned the proverb to its own use, well convinced that in its mouth, *repetition teaches.*

The advantages which officials advocate are those which are seen. The benefit which accrues to the suppliers is still that which is seen.

This blinds all eyes.

The disadvantages which burden the tax-payers are not seen. And the injury which results from this burden to their suppliers is still that which is not seen, although this ought to be self-evident.

When an official spends for his own benefit an extra hundred *sous*, it implies that a tax-payer spends for his benefit a hundred *sous* less. But the expenditure of the official is seen because the act is performed, while that of the tax-payer is not seen because, alas! he is prevented from performing it.

You compare the nation, perhaps to a parched tract of land and the tax to a fertilising rain. Be it so. But you ought also to ask yourself where are the sources of this rain, and whether it is not the tax itself which draws away the moisture from the ground and dries it up?

Again, you ought to ask yourself whether it is possible that the soil can receive as much of this precious water by rain as it loses by evaporation?

There is one thing very certain, that when James Goodman counts out a hundred *sous* for the tax-gatherer, he receives nothing in return. Afterwards, when an official spends these hundred *sous*, and returns them to James Goodman it is for an equal value in corn or labour. The final result is a loss to James Goodman of one hundred *sous*.[5]

It is very true that often, perhaps very often, the official performs for James Goodman an equivalent service. In this case there is no loss on either side; there is merely an exchange. Therefore, my arguments do not at all apply to useful functionaries. All I say is, if you wish to create an office, prove its utility. Show that its value to James Goodman, by the services which it performs for him, is equal to what it costs him.

But, apart from this intrinsic utility, do not bring forward as an argument the benefit which it confers upon the official, his family, and his suppliers; do not assert that it aids employment.

When James Goodman gives a hundred *sous* to a Government officer for a really useful service, it is exactly the same as when he gives a hundred *sous* to a shoemaker for a pair of shoes.

---

5   In effect and in a roundabout way, the money extracted through tax from James Goodman was used to pay for the supplies or services the government bought from him.

But when James Goodman gives a hundred *sous* to a Government officer, and receives nothing for them unless it be annoyances, he might as well give them to a thief. It is nonsense to say that the Government officer will spend these hundred *sous* to the great profit of national productivity. The thief would do the same; and so would James Goodman, if he had not been stopped on the road by the extra-legal parasite, nor by the lawful sponger.

Let us accustom ourselves, then, to avoid judging of things by what is seen only, but to judge them by that which is not seen.

Last year I was on the Committee of Finance, for under the constituency the members of the Opposition were not systematically excluded from all the Commissions: in that the constituency acted wisely. We have heard Monsieur Thiers say, "I have passed my life in opposing the legitimist party[6] and the priest party.[7] Since the common danger has brought us together, now that I associate with them and know them, and now that we speak face to face, I have found out that they are not the monsters I used to imagine them."

Yes, distrust is exaggerated, hatred is fostered among parties who never mix; and if the majority would allow the minority to be present at the Commissions, it would perhaps be discovered that the ideas of the different sides are not so far removed from each other; and, above all, that their intentions are not as perverse as is supposed. However, last year I was on the Committee of Finance. Every time that one of our colleagues spoke of fixing at a moderate figure the maintenance of the President of the Republic, that of the

---

6 The Legitimist party favoured royal lineage and was thus counter-revolutionary.

7 A reference to the Assembly of the Clergy—an influential Catholic group which liaised with the French state.

ministers, and of the ambassadors, it was answered:

> "For the good of the service, it is necessary to surround
> certain offices with splendour and dignity, as a means
> of attracting men of merit to them. A vast number
> of unfortunate persons apply to the President of the
> Republic, and it would be placing him in a very painful
> position to oblige him to be constantly refusing them.
> A certain style in the ministerial saloons is a part of the
> machinery of constitutional Governments."

Although such arguments may be controverted, they certainly
deserve a serious examination. They are based upon the public
interest, whether rightly estimated or not; and as far as I am
concerned, I have much more respect for them than many of our
Catos[8] have who are actuated by a narrow spirit of parsimony or
of jealousy.

But what revolts the economical part of my conscience, and makes
me blush for the intellectual resources of my country, is when this
absurd relic of feudalism is brought forward, which it constantly is
and is favourably received too:

> "Besides, the luxury of great Government officers
> encourages the arts, industry, and labour. The head of
> the State and his ministers cannot give banquets and
> soirées without causing life to circulate through all the
> veins of the social body. To reduce their means, would
> starve Parisian industry, and consequently that of the
> whole nation."

---

8   Cato the Younger and Cato the Elder: two shrewd Senators in Imperial Rome.

I must beg you gentlemen to pay some little regard to arithmetic at least; and not to say before the National Assembly in France, lest to its shame it should agree with you, that an addition gives a different sum according to whether it is added up from the bottom to the top, or from the top to the bottom of the column.

For instance, I want to deal with a drainer to make a trench in my field for a hundred *sous*. Just as we have concluded our arrangement the tax-gatherer comes, takes my hundred *sous* and sends them to the Minister of the Interior. My dealings with the drainer are at end, but the minister will have another dish added to his table. Upon what ground will you dare to affirm that this official expense helps the national industry? Do you not see that in this there is only a reversing of satisfaction and labour? A minister has his table better covered, it is true; but it is just as true that an agriculturist has his field worse drained. A Parisian tavern-keeper has gained a hundred *sous*, I grant you; but then you must grant me that a drainer has been prevented from gaining a hundred *sous*.

It all comes to this: that the official and the tavern-keeper being satisfied is that which is seen; the field undrained and the drainer deprived of his job is that which is not seen. Dear me! How much trouble there is in proving that two and two make four, and if you succeed in proving it, it is said "The thing is so plain it is quite tiresome," and they vote as if you had proved nothing at all.

4. Theatres, Fine Arts

Ought the State to support the arts? There is certainly much to be said on both sides of this question. It may be said, in favour of the system of voting supplies for this purpose, that the arts enlarge, elevate, and harmonize the soul of a nation; that they divert it from too great an absorption in material occupations; encourage in it a love for the beautiful; and thus act favourably on its manners, customs, morals, and even on its industry. It may be asked, what would become of music in France without her Italian theatre and her Conservatoire; of the dramatic art, without her Théâtre-Français[9]; of painting and sculpture, without our collections, galleries, and museums? It might even be asked, whether, without centralisation, and consequently the support of the fine arts, that exquisite taste would be developed which is the noble appendage of French labour, and which introduces its productions to the whole world?

In the face of such results, would it not be the height of imprudence to renounce this moderate contribution from all her citizens, which, in fact, in the eyes of Europe, realises their superiority and their glory?

To these and many other reasons, whose force I do not dispute, arguments no less forcible may be opposed. It might first of all be said that there is a question of distributive justice in it. Does the right of the legislator extend to abridging the wages of the tradespeople, for the sake of adding to the profits of the artist?

---

9   Theatre-Francais: French national theatre group, headquarter in Paris, supported by the State.

Monsieur Lamartine[10] said,

> "If you cease to support the theatre, where will you
> stop? Will you not necessarily be led to withdraw
> your support from your colleges, your museums, your
> institutes, and your libraries?"

It might be answered, if you desire *to support* everything which
is good and useful, where will you stop? Will you not necessarily
be led to form subsidies for agriculture, industry, commerce,
benevolence, education? Then, is it certain that Government aid
favours the progress of art?

This question is far from being settled, and we see very well that
the theatres which prosper are those which depend upon their
own resources. Moreover, if we come to higher considerations,
we may observe that wants and desires arise the one from the
other, and originate in regions which are more and more refined in
proportion as the public wealth allows of their being satisfied; that
Government ought not to take part in this correspondence, because
in a certain condition of present fortune it could not by taxation
stimulate the arts of necessity without checking those of luxury,
and thus interrupting the natural course of civilisation. I may
observe that these artificial displacements of wants, tastes, labour,
and population, place the people in a precarious and dangerous
position, without any solid basis.

These are some of the reasons advanced by the adversaries of State
intervention in what concerns the order in which citizens think their
wants and desires should be satisfied and to which, consequently,

---

10 Alphonse de Lamartine (1790-1869) influential French statesman, writer,
supporter of the arts.

their activity should be directed. I am, I confess, one of those who think that choice and impulse ought to come from below and not from above, from the citizen and not from the legislator; and the opposite doctrine appears to me to tend to the destruction of liberty and of human dignity.

But, by a deduction as false as it is unjust, do you know what economists are accused of? It is that when we disapprove of government support, we are supposed to disapprove of the thing itself whose support is discussed; and to be the enemies of every kind of activity, because we desire to see those activities, on the one hand free, and on the other seeking their own reward in themselves.

Thus, if we think that the State should not interfere by taxation in religious affairs, we are atheists. If we think the State ought not to interfere by taxation in education, we are hostile to knowledge. If we say that the State ought not by taxation to give a fictitious value to land, or to any particular branch of industry, we are enemies to property and labour. If we think that the State ought not to support artists, we are barbarians who look upon the arts as useless.

Against such conclusions as these I protest with all my strength. Far from entertaining the absurd idea of doing away with religion, education, property, labour, and the arts, when we say that the State ought to protect the free development of all these kinds of human activity, without helping some of them at the expense of others— we think, on the contrary, that all these living powers of society would develop themselves more harmoniously under the influence of liberty; and that, under such an influence not one of them would, as is now the case, be a source of trouble, of abuses, of tyranny, and disorder.

Our adversaries consider that an activity which is neither aided by subsidies, nor regulated by government, is an activity destroyed. We think just the contrary. Their faith is in the legislator, not in mankind; ours is in mankind, not in the legislator.

Thus Monsieur Lamartine said, "Upon this principle we must abolish the public exhibitions, which are the honour and the wealth of this country!"

But I would say to M. Lamartine: According to your way of thinking, not to support is to abolish; because, setting out upon the maxim that nothing exists independently of the will of the State, you conclude that nothing lives but what the State causes to live. But I oppose to this assertion the very example which you have chosen, and beg you to notice that the grandest and noblest of exhibitions, one which has been conceived in the most liberal and universal spirit—and I might even make use of the term *humanitarian*, for it is no exaggeration—is the exhibition now preparing in London; the only one in which no government is taking any part, and which is being paid for by no tax.

To return to the fine arts. There are, I repeat, many strong reasons to be brought, both for and against the system of government assistance. The reader must see that the object of this work leads me neither to explain these reasons, nor to decide in their favour, nor against them.

But M. Lamartine has advanced one argument which I cannot pass by in silence, for it is closely connected with this economic study.

> "The economical question, as regards theatres, is comprised in one word—labour. It matters little what

is the nature of this labour; it is as fertile, as productive a labour as any other kind of labour in the nation. The theatres in France, you know, feed and salary no less than 80,000 workmen of different kinds; painters, masons, decorators, costumers, architects, etc., which constitute the very life and movement of several parts of this capital, and on this account they ought to have your sympathies."

Your sympathies! Say rather your money!

And further on he says:

"The pleasures of Paris are the labour and the consumption of the provinces, and the luxuries of the rich are the wages and bread of 200,000 workmen of every description, who live by the manifold industry of the theatres on the surface of the republic, and who receive from these noble pleasures, which render France illustrious, the sustenance of their lives and the necessaries of their families and children. It is to them that you will give 60,000 *francs*." (Very well; very well. Great applause.)

For my part I am constrained to say, "Very bad! Very bad!" Confining this opinion, of course, within the bounds of the economic question which we are discussing.

Yes, it is to the workmen of the theatres that a part, at least, of these 60,000 *francs* will go; a few bribes, perhaps, may be abstracted on the way. Perhaps, if we were to look a little more closely into the matter, we might find that the cake had gone another way and that those workmen were fortunate who had come in for a few crumbs.

But I will allow, for the sake of argument, that the entire sum does go to the painters, decorators, etc.

This is that which is seen. But whence does it come? This is the other side of the question, and quite as important as the former. Where do these 60,000 *francs* spring from? and where would they go, if a vote of the legislature did not direct them first towards the Rue Rivoli and thence towards the Rue Grenelle?[11] This is what is not seen. Certainly, nobody will think of maintaining that the legislative vote has caused this sum to be hatched in a ballot urn; that it is a pure addition made to the national wealth; that but for this miraculous vote these 60,000 *francs* would have been for ever invisible and impalpable. It must be admitted that all that the majority can do is to decide that the money shall be taken from one place to be sent to another; and if they take one direction, it is only because they have been diverted from another.

This being the case, it is clear that the tax-payer, who has contributed one *franc*, will no longer have this *franc* at his disposal. It is clear that he will be deprived of some gratification to the amount of one *franc*; and that the workman, whoever he may be, who would have received it from him, will be deprived of a benefit to that amount. Let us not, therefore, be led by a childish illusion into believing that the vote of the 60,000 *francs* may add anything whatever to the well-being of the country and to national labour. It displaces enjoyments, it transposes wages: that is all.

Will it be said that for one kind of gratification, and one kind of labour, it substitutes more urgent, more moral, more reasonable gratifications and labour? I might dispute this; I might say, by

---

11 Two Parisian streets: the Ministry of Finances was located in the Rue de Rivoli; the Ministry of Fine Arts in the Rue de Grenelle.

taking 60,000 *francs* from the tax-payers, you diminish the wages of labourers, drainers, carpenters, blacksmiths, and increase in proportion those of the singers.

There is nothing to prove that this latter class calls for more sympathy than the former. M. Lamartine does not say that it is so. He himself says that the labour of the theatres is as fertile, as productive as any other (not more so). But this may be doubted; for the best proof that the latter is not so fertile as the former lies in this: that the other is to be called upon to assist it.

But this comparison between the value and the intrinsic merit of different kinds of labour forms no part of my present subject. All I have to do here is to show that if M. Lamartine and those persons who commend his line of argument have seen on one side the salaries gained by the providers of the comedians, they ought on the other to have seen the salaries lost by the providers of the tax-payers: for want of this, they have exposed themselves to ridicule by mistaking a displacement for a gain. If they were true to their doctrine, there would be no limits to their demands for government aid; for that which is true of one *franc* and of 60,000 is true, under parallel circumstances, of a hundred millions of *francs*.

When taxes are the subject of discussion, you ought to prove their utility by reasons from the root of the matter, but not by this unlucky assertion: "The public expenses support the working classes." This assertion disguises the important fact that public expenses always supersede private expenses, and that therefore we bring a livelihood to one workman instead of another, but add nothing to the share of the working class as a whole. Your arguments are fashionable enough, but they are too absurd to be justified by anything like reason.

5. Public Works

Nothing is more natural than that a nation, after having assured itself that an enterprise will benefit the community, should have it executed by means of a general subscription.[12] But I lose patience, I confess, when I hear this economic blunder advanced in support of such a project: "Besides, it will be a means of creating labour for the workmen."

The State opens a road, builds a palace, straightens a street, cuts a canal, and so gives work to certain workmen, this is what is seen: but it deprives certain other workmen of work, and this is what is not seen.

The road is begun. A thousand workmen come every morning, leave every evening, and take their wages: this is certain. If the road had not been decreed, if the supplies had not been voted, these good people would have had neither work nor salary *there*; this also is certain.

But is this all? Does not the operation, as a whole, contain something else? At the moment when Monsieur Dupin[13] pronounces the emphatic words, "The Assembly has adopted," do the millions descend miraculously on a moonbeam into the coffers of Monsieur

---

12 General subscription is yet another form of taxation.

13 André Marie Jean Jacques Dupin (1783-1865) French statesman, President of the Chamber of Deputies for seven years.

Fould[14] and Monsieur Bineau?[15] In order that the project may be completed, as it is said, must not the State organise the tax receipts as well as the expenditure? Must it not set its tax-gatherers and tax-payers to work, the former to gather and the latter to pay?

Study the question, now, in both its elements. While you announce the destination given by the State to the millions of *francs* voted, do not neglect to announce also the destination which the tax-payer would have given, but cannot now give, to the same amount. Then you will understand that a public enterprise is a coin with two sides. Upon one is engraved a labourer at work, with this mark: *that which is seen*; on the other is a labourer out of work, with the mark: *that which is not seen*.

The sophism which this book is intended to refute is the more dangerous when applied to public works, inasmuch as it serves to justify the most wanton enterprises and extravagance. When a railroad or a bridge is of real utility, it is sufficient to mention this utility. But if its utility does not exist, what do they do? Recourse is had to this mystification: "We must find work for the workmen."

Accordingly, orders are given that the drains in the Champ-de-Mars be made and unmade. The great Napoleon, it is said, thought he was doing a very philanthropic work by causing ditches to be made and then filled up. He said, therefore, "What signifies the result? All we want is to see wealth spread among the labouring classes."

But let us go to the root of the matter. We are deceived by money. To demand the co-operation of all the citizens in a common work,

14 Achille Fould (1800-1867) French financier and politician.

15 Jean Martial Bineau (1805-1855) was at different times French minister of finance, minister of public works.

in the form of money, is in reality to demand a concurrence in kind; for every one procures, by his own labour, the sum to which he is taxed. Now, if all the citizens were to be called together and made to execute, in conjunction, a work useful to all, this would be easily understood; their reward would be found in the results of the work itself.

But after having called them together, if you force them to make roads which no one will pass through, palaces which no one will inhabit, and this under the pretext of finding them work, it would be absurd, and they would have a right to argue, "With this labour we have nothing to do; we prefer working on our own account!"

A project which consists in making the citizens co-operate in giving money but not labour, does not, in any way, alter the general results. The only thing is that the loss would react upon all parties. By the former, those whom the State employs, escape their part of the loss, by adding it to that which their fellow-citizens have already suffered.[16]

There is an article in our constitution which says:

> "Society favours and encourages the development of labour, by the establishment of public works, by the State, the departments, and the parishes, as a means of employing persons who are in want of work."

As a temporary measure, on any emergency, during a hard winter, this interference with the tax-payers may have its use. It acts in the same way as securities. It adds nothing either to labour or to wages, but it takes labour and wages from ordinary times to give them, at

---

16 State employees receive their wages no matter the absurdities that politicians impose on the tax-payer.

a loss it is true, to times of difficulty.

As a permanent, general, systematic measure, it is nothing else than a ruinous mystification, an impossibility, which shows a little stimulated labour—which is seen—and hides a great deal of prevented labour which is not seen.

6. The Intermediaries

Society is the total of the forced or voluntary services which men perform for each other; that is to say, of public services and private services. Public services, imposed and regulated by the law, which it is not always easy to change, even when change is desirable, may outlive their own usefulness and still preserve the name of public services even when they are no longer services at all, but rather public annoyances. Private services belong to the sphere of the will, of individual responsibility. Every one gives and receives what he wishes, and what he can, after a debate. They have always the presumption of real utility, in exact proportion to their comparative value.

This is the reason why the former, legislated services, so often become stationary, while the latter, private services, confirm the law of progress.

While the exaggerated development of public services, by the waste of strength which it involves, fastens upon society a fatal sycophancy, it is a singular thing that several modern sects, attributing this character to free and private services, are endeavouring to transform professionals into state functionaries.

These sects violently oppose what they call intermediaries. They would gladly suppress the capitalist, the banker, the speculator, the projector, the merchant, and the trader, accusing them of interposing between production and consumption, to extort from both, without giving either anything in return. Or rather, they would transfer to the State the work which they accomplish, for this work cannot be avoided.

The sophism of the Socialists on this point is, showing to the public what it pays to the intermediaries in exchange for their services, and concealing from it what is necessary to be paid to the State. Here is the usual conflict between what is before our eyes and what is perceptible to the mind only; between what is seen and what is not seen.

It was at the time of the scarcity, in 1847[17] that the Socialist schools attempted and succeeded in popularizing their fatal theory. They knew very well that the most absurd notions have always a chance with people who are suffering; *malisunda fames.*[18]

Therefore, by the help of the fine words, "Trafficking in men by men! Speculation on hunger! Monopoly!" they began to blacken commerce, and to cast a veil over its benefits.

> "What can be the use," they say, "of leaving to the merchants the care of importing food from the United States and the Crimea? Why do not the State, the departments, and the towns, organize a service for provisions and warehouses for stores? They would sell at a return price, and the people, poor things, would be exempted from the burden which they pay to free trade, that is, to egotistical, individual, and anarchical commerce."

The money paid by the people to commerce is that which is seen.

---

17 Widespread crop failures created food shortages.

18 Latin: driven to evil by hunger.

The money which the people would pay to the State, or to its agents, in the Socialist system, is what is not seen.

In what does this pretended burden, which the people pay to commerce, consist? In this: that two men render each other a mutual service, in all freedom, and under the pressure of competition and reduced prices.

When the hungry stomach is at Paris, and corn which can satisfy it is at Odessa,[19] the suffering cannot cease till the corn is brought into contact with the stomach. There are three means by which this contact may be effected:

1. The famished men may go themselves and fetch the corn.

2. They may leave this task to those to who specialise.

3. They may club together, and give the task to public functionaries.

Which of these three methods possesses the greatest advantages? In every time, in all countries, and the more free, enlightened, and experienced they are, men have voluntarily chosen the second. I confess that this is sufficient, in my opinion, to justify this choice. I cannot believe that mankind, as a whole, is deceiving itself upon a point which touches it so nearly. But let us now consider the subject.

For thirty-six millions of citizens to go and fetch the corn they want from Odessa, is a manifest impossibility. The first method, then, goes for nothing. The consumers cannot act for themselves. They must, of necessity, have recourse to intermediates, officials or agents.

---

19 Odessa: major port of Ukraine, formerly Russian.

But notice: that the first of these three methods would be the most natural. In reality, the hungry man has to fetch his corn. It is a task which concerns himself, a service due to himself. If another person, on whatever ground, performs this service for him, takes the task upon himself, this latter has a claim upon him for a compensation. I mean by this to say that intermediaries contain in themselves the principle of remuneration.

However that may be, since we must refer to what the Socialists call a parasite, I would ask, which of the two is the most exacting parasite: the merchant or the official?

Commerce (free, of course, otherwise I could not reason upon it), commerce, I say, is led by its own interests to study the seasons, to give daily statements of the state of the crops, to receive information from every part of the globe, to foresee wants, to take precautions beforehand. It has vessels always ready, correspondents everywhere; and its immediate interest is to buy at the lowest possible price, to economize in all the details of its operations, and to attain the greatest results by the smallest efforts. It is not the French merchants only who are occupied in procuring provisions for France in time of need, and if their interest leads them irresistibly to accomplish their task at the smallest possible cost, the competition which they create amongst each other leads them no less irresistibly to cause the consumers to partake of the profits of those realised savings. The corn arrives: it is to the interest of commerce to sell it as soon as possible, so as to avoid risks, to realise its funds, and begin again at the first opportunity.

Directed by the comparison of prices, it distributes food over the whole surface of the country, beginning always at the highest price, that is, where the demand is the greatest. It is impossible to imagine an organisation more completely calculated to meet the interest of those who are in want; and the beauty of this organisation, unperceived as it is by the Socialists, results from the very fact that it is free. It is true, the consumer is obliged to reimburse merchants for the expenses of conveyance, freight, store-room, commission, etc., but can any system be devised in which he who eats corn is not obliged to defray the expenses, whatever they may be, of bringing it within his reach? The remuneration for the service performed has to be paid also; but as regards its amount, this is reduced to the smallest possible sum by competition; and as regards its justice, it would be very strange if the artisans of Paris would not work for the artisans of Marseilles,[20] when the merchants of Marseilles work for the artisans of Paris.

If, according to the Socialist invention, the State were to stand in the stead of merchants, what would happen? I should like to be informed, where the saving would be to the public? Would it be in the price of purchase? Imagine the delegates of 40,000 parishes arriving at Odessa on a given day, and on the day of need: imagine the effect upon prices! Would the saving be in the expenses? Would fewer vessels be required; fewer sailors, fewer transports, fewer sloops? Or would you be exempt from the payment of all these things? Would it be in the profits of the merchants? Would your officials go to Odessa for nothing? Would they travel and work on the principle of fraternity? Must they not live? Must not they be paid for their time? And do you believe that these expenses would not exceed a thousand times the two or three per cent., which the merchant gains—the rate at which he is ready to begin his work?

And then consider the difficulty of levying so many taxes and

---

20 Marseilles, major French port city on Mediterranean coast.

of dividing so much food. Think of the injustice, of the abuses inseparable from such an enterprise. Think of the responsibility which would weigh upon the Government.

The Socialists who have invented these follies, and who, in the days of distress, have introduced them into the minds of the masses, take to themselves literally the title of advanced men; and it is not without some danger that custom, that tyrant of tongues, authorizes the term and the sentiment which it involves. Advanced!

This supposes that these gentlemen can see further than the common people; that their only fault is that they are too much in advance of their age; and if the time is not yet come for suppressing certain free services, pretended parasites,[21] the fault is to be attributed to the public which is in the rear of Socialism.

I say, from my soul and my conscience, the reverse is the truth; and I know not to what barbarous age we should have to go back, if we would find the level of Socialist knowledge on this subject. These modern sectarians incessantly oppose association[22] to actual society. They overlook the fact that society, under a free regulation, is a true association, far superior to any of those which proceed from their fertile imaginations.

Let me illustrate this by an example. Before any mutual service, as people help each other in a common object and admitting all the complex tasks that must be done, intermediaries are required. If, for instance, in the course of the operation, the transportation of goods becomes important enough to occupy one person, spinning

---

21 Bastiat mockingly echoes the accusation of the socialists against the merchants.

22 *Association* was a socialist catch-cry, here contrasted by Bastiat with freely chosen co-operation.

another, and weaving another, why should the first be considered a parasite more than the other two? Transportation must be made, must it not? Does not he who performs it devote to it his time and trouble? And by so doing does he not spare that of his colleagues?

Do these do more or other than this for him? Are they not equally dependent for remuneration, that is, for the division of the produce, upon the law of reduced price? Is it not in all liberty, for the common good, that this separation of work takes place, and that these arrangements are entered into? What do we want with a Socialist then, who, under pretence of organising for us, comes despotically to break up our voluntary arrangements, to check the division of labour, to substitute isolated efforts for combined ones, and to send civilisation back? Is association, as I describe it here, in itself less association, because everyone enters and leaves it freely, chooses his place in it, judges and bargains for himself on his own responsibility, and brings with him the spring and warrant of personal interest? That it may deserve this name, is it necessary that a pretended reformer should come and impose upon us his plan and his will, and, as it were, to concentrate mankind in himself?

The more we examine these advanced schools, the more do we become convinced that there is but one thing at the root of them: ignorance proclaiming itself infallible, and claiming despotism in the name of this infallibility.

I hope the reader will excuse this digression. It may not be altogether useless, at a time when declamations, springing from St. Simonian,[23]

---

23 Claude Henri de Rouvroy, comte de Saint-Simon (1760–1825) was the founder of French socialism.

Phalansterian,[24] and Icarian[25] books, are invoking the press and the tribune, and which seriously threaten the liberty of labour and commercial transactions.

24 Phalanstery was a type of Utopian socialist community promoted by Charles Fourier (1772-1837).

25 Icaria, fictional country: a perfect Communist world described in a book by French socialist Etienne Cabet (1788-1856).

7. Restrictions

Monsieur Prohibant[26] (it was not I who gave him this name, but Monsieur Charles Dupin) devoted his time and capital to converting the ore found on his land into iron. As nature had been more lavish towards the Belgians, they furnished the French with iron cheaper than M. Prohibant; which means, that all the French, or France, could obtain a given quantity of iron with less labour by buying it from the honest Belgians. Therefore, guided by their own interest, they did not fail to do so. Every day there might be seen a multitude of nail-smiths, blacksmiths, cartwrights, machinists, farriers, and labourers, going themselves, or sending intermediaries, to supply themselves in Belgium. This displeased M. Prohibant exceedingly.

At first, it occurred to him to put an end to this abuse by his own efforts: it was the least he could do, for he was the only sufferer. "I will take my carbine," said he. "I will put four pistols into my belt; I will fill my cartridge box; I will gird on my sword, and go thus equipped to the Belgian frontier. There, the first blacksmith, nail-smith, farrier, machinist, or locksmith, who presents himself to do his own business and not mine, I will kill, to teach him how to live."

At the moment of starting, M. Prohibant made a few reflections which calmed down his warlike ardour a little. He said to himself,

---

26 Mocking name for protectionist: Mister Prohibiter. First used by Charles Dupin, a free market economist.

"In the first place, it is not absolutely impossible that the purchasers of iron, my countrymen and enemies, should take the thing ill and, instead of letting me kill them, should kill me instead; and then, even were I to call out all my servants, we should not be able to defend the passages. In short, this proceeding would cost me very dear, much more so than the result would be worth."

M. Prohibant was on the point of resigning himself to his sad fate, that of being only as free as the rest of the world, when a ray of light darted across his brain. He recollected that at Paris there is a great manufactory of laws.[27]

"What is a law?" said he to himself. "It is a measure to which, when once it is decreed, be it good or bad, everybody is bound to conform. To impose the law a public force is organised, and to constitute this public force, men and money are drawn from the whole nation. If, then, I could only get the great Parisian manufactory to pass a little law, 'Belgian iron is prohibited,' I should obtain the following results: The Government would replace the few servants that I was going to send to the frontier by 20,000 of the sons of those refractory blacksmiths, farriers, artisans, machinists, locksmiths, nail-smiths, and labourers. Then to keep these 20,000 custom-house officers in health and good humour, it would distribute among them 25,000,000 of *francs* taken from these blacksmiths, nail-smiths, artisans, and labourers. They would guard the frontier much better; would cost me nothing; I should not be exposed to the brutality of the brokers; should sell the iron at my own price, and have the sweet satisfaction of seeing our great people shamefully mystified. That would teach them to proclaim themselves perpetually the innovators and promoters of progress in Europe. Oh! it would be a

---

27   Bastiat refers to the French National Assembly.

capital joke, and deserves to be tried."

So M. Prohibant went to the law manufactory. Another time, perhaps, I shall relate the story of his underhand dealings, but now I shall merely mention his visible proceedings. He brought the following consideration before the view of the legislating gentlemen.

> "Belgian iron is sold in France at ten *francs*, which obliges me to sell mine at the same price. I should like to sell at fifteen, but cannot do so on account of this Belgian iron, which I wish was at the bottom of the Red Sea. I beg you will make a law that no more Belgian iron shall enter France. Immediately I raise my price five *francs*, and these are the consequences:

> "For every hundred-weight of iron that I shall deliver to the public, I shall receive fifteen *francs* instead of ten; I shall grow rich more rapidly, extend my traffic, and employ more workmen. My workmen and I shall spend much more freely, to the great advantage of our tradesmen for miles around. These latter, having more custom, will furnish more employment to trade, and activity on both sides will increase in the country. This fortunate piece of money, which you will drop into my strong-box, will, like a stone thrown into a lake, give birth to an infinite number of concentric circles."

Charmed with his discourse, delighted to learn that it is so easy to promote—by legislating—the prosperity of a people, the lawmakers voted the restriction. "Talk of labour and economy," they said, "what is the use of these painful means of increasing the national wealth, when all that is wanted for this object is a law?"

And, in fact, the law produced all the consequences announced by M. Prohibant: the only thing was it also produced others which he had not foreseen. To do him justice, his reasoning was not false, but only incomplete. In endeavouring to obtain a privilege, he had taken note of the effects which are seen, leaving in the background those which are not seen. He had pointed out only two of the persons involved, whereas there are three concerned in the affair. It is for us to supply this involuntary—or premeditated—omission.

It is true, the money thus directed by law into M. Prohibant's strong-box is advantageous to him and to those whose labour it would encourage. And if the Act had caused the money to descend from the moon, these good effects would not have been counterbalanced by any corresponding evils. Unfortunately, the mysterious money does not come from the moon, but from the pocket of a blacksmith, or silver-smith, or a cartwright, or a farrier, or a labourer, or a shipwright; in a word, from James Goodman, who gives it now without receiving anymore iron than when he was paying ten *francs*. Thus, we can see at a glance that this very much alters the state of the case; for it is very evident that M. Prohibant's *profit* is compensated by James Goodman's *loss*, and all that M. Prohibant can do with the money for the encouragement of national labour, James Goodman might have done himself.

The stone has only been thrown upon one part of the lake, because the law has prevented it from being thrown upon another.

Therefore, that which is not seen supersedes that which is seen, and at this point there remains, as the residue of the operation, a piece of injustice and, sad to say, a piece of injustice perpetrated by the law!

This is not all. I have said that there is always a third person left in the background. I must now bring him forward, that he may reveal to us a second loss of five *francs*. Then we shall have the entire results of the transaction.

Before the new decree: James Goodman is the possessor of fifteen *francs*, the fruit of his labour. He is now free. What does he do with his fifteen *francs*? He purchases some *Article de Paris*[28] for ten *francs*, and with it he pays (or the intermediary pays for him) for the hundred-weight of Belgian iron. After this he has five *francs* left. He does not throw them into the river, but (and this is what is not seen) he gives them to some tradesman in exchange for some enjoyment; to a bookseller, for instance, for Bossuet's "Discourse on Universal History."

Thus, as far as national labour is concerned, it is encouraged to the amount of fifteen *francs*, that is, ten *francs* for the *Article de Paris*, five *francs* to the bookselling trade.

As to James Goodman, he obtains for his fifteen *francs* two gratifications, which are:

    1. A hundred-weight of iron.
    2. A book.

The restrictive decree is put in force. How does it affect the condition of James Goodman? How does it affect the national labour?

James Goodman pays his extra five *francs* to M. Prohibant, and therefore is deprived of the pleasure of a book, or of some other thing of equal value. He loses five *francs*. This must be admitted; it cannot fail to be admitted that when the restriction raises the price of things, the consumer loses the difference.

---

28 Fashionable accessory, including household accoutrements.

But then it is said, *national productivity* is the gainer.

No, it is not the gainer; for after the Act it is no more encouraged than it was before to the amount of fifteen *francs*.

The only thing is that, *since the Act*, the fifteen *francs* of James Goodman go to the metal trade, while *before the Act* they were divided between the milliner and the bookseller.

The violence used by M. Prohibant on the frontier, or that which he causes to be used by the law, may be judged very differently in a moral point of view. Some persons consider that plunder is perfectly justifiable, if only sanctioned by law. But, for myself, I cannot imagine anything more aggravating. However it may be, the economical results are the same in both cases.

Look at the thing as you will; but if you are impartial, you will see that no good can come of legal or illegal plunder. We do not deny that it affords M. Prohibant or his trade or, if you will, national industry a profit of five *francs*. But we affirm that it causes two losses: one to James Goodman, who pays fifteen *francs* where he otherwise would have paid ten; the other to national industry, which does not receive the five *francs* difference. Take your choice of these two losses,[29] and compensate with it the profit which we allow. The other will prove not the less a dead loss.

Here is the moral: *To take by violence is not to produce, but to destroy.* Truly, if taking by violence was productive, this country of ours would be a little richer than she is.

---

29 James Goodman suffers a five *francs* loss, and so does the milliner or book-seller in the foregone sale. Mr Prohibant alone gains the profit of five *francs*. He may indeed spend it at the milliner's or bookshop. Overall, economic activity is the same but a serious injustice has been perpetrated.

8. Machinery

"A curse on machines! Every year, their increasing power condemns millions of workmen to pauperism, by depriving them of work, and therefore of wages and bread. A curse on machines!"

This is the cry which is raised by vulgar prejudice, and echoed in the journals.

But to curse machines is to curse the spirit of humanity! It puzzles me to conceive how any man can feel any satisfaction in such a doctrine.

For, if true, what is its inevitable consequence? That there is no activity, prosperity, wealth, or happiness possible for any people, except for those who are stupid and inert, and to whom God has *not* granted the fatal gift of knowing how to think, to observe, to combine, to invent, and to obtain the greatest results with the smallest means.

Are we to believe that rags, mean huts, poverty, and inanition, are the inevitable lot of every nation which seeks and finds in iron, fire, wind, electricity, magnetism, the laws of chemistry and mechanics, in a word, in the powers of nature, an assistance to its natural powers? We might as well say with Rousseau,[30] "Every man that thinks is a depraved animal."

---

30 Jean-Jacques Rousseau (1712-1778), a writer, believed civilisation ruins humanity. His call was to return to nature.

This is not all. If this doctrine is true since all men think and invent, since all from first to last and at every moment of their existence, seek the co-operation of the powers of nature and try to make the most of a little, by reducing either the work of their hands or their expenses, so as to obtain the greatest possible amount of gratification with the smallest possible amount of labour, it must follow, as a matter of course, that the whole of mankind is rushing towards its decline, by the same mental aspiration towards progress which torments each of its members.

Hence, it ought to be revealed by statistics, that the inhabitants of Lancashire, abandoning that land of machines, seek for work in Ireland, where they are unknown; and, by history, that barbarism darkens the epochs of civilisation, and that civilisation shines in times of ignorance and barbarism.

There is evidently in this mass of contradictions something which revolts us, and which leads us to suspect that the problem contains within it an element of solution which has been overlooked.

Here is the whole mystery: behind that which is seen lies something which is not seen. I will endeavour to bring it to light. The demonstration I shall give will only be a repetition of the preceding one, for the problems are one and the same.

Men have a natural propensity to make the best bargain they can when not prevented by an opposing force; that is, they like to obtain as much as they possibly can for their labour, whether the advantage is obtained from a foreign producer or innovative mechanical production.

The theoretical objection which is made to this propensity is the same in both cases. In each case it is reproached with the apparent inactivity which it causes to labour. Now, labour rendered *available*, not inactive, is the very thing which is gained. But, in both cases, the same practical obstacle—legislated force—comes to restrict mechanical innovation.

The legislator prohibits foreign competition,[31] and forbids mechanical competition. For what other means can exist for arresting a propensity which is natural to all men, but that of depriving them of their liberty?

In many countries, it is true, the legislator strikes at only one of these competitions, and confines himself to grumbling at the other. This only proves one thing, that is, that the legislator is inconsistent.

We need not be surprised at this. On a wrong road, inconsistency is inevitable; if it were not so, mankind would be sacrificed. A false principle never has been, and never will be, carried out to the end.

Now for our demonstration, which shall not be a long one:

James Goodman had two *francs* which he had gained by two workmen; but it occurs to him that an arrangement of ropes and weights might be made which would diminish the labour by half. Therefore he obtains the same advantage, saves a *franc*, and discharges a workman.

He discharges a workman: this is that which is seen.

And seeing this only, it is said, "See how misery attends civilisation; this is the way that liberty is fatal to equality. The human mind has made a successful invention, and immediately a workman is cast

---

31 See *Petition of the Candlemakers* for Bastiat's position on trade restrictions.

into the gulf of pauperism. James Goodman may possibly employ the two workmen, but then he will give them only half their wages, for they will compete with each other and offer themselves at the lowest price. Thus the rich are always growing richer, and the poor, poorer. Society wants remodelling."[32]

A very fine conclusion, and worthy of the preamble!

Happily, preamble and conclusion are both false, because behind the half of the phenomenon which is seen lies the other half which is not seen.

The *franc* saved by James Goodman is not seen, neither are the necessary effects of this saving.

Since, in consequence of his invention, James Goodman spends only one *franc* on labour in the pursuit of a determined advantage, another *franc* remains to him.

If, then, there is in the world an unemployed workman, there is also in the world a capitalist with an unemployed *franc*. These two elements meet and combine, and it is as clear as daylight, that between the supply and demand of labour, and between the supply and demand of wages, the relation is in no way changed.

The invention and the workman paid with the first *franc*, now perform the work which was formerly accomplished by two workmen. The second workman, paid with the second *franc*, undertakes a different kind of work.

What is the change, then, which has taken place? There has been a gain in national production; in other words, the invention is a

---

32 Bastiat repeats the arguments of the Socialists.

gratuitous triumph: a gratuitous profit for mankind.

From the form which I have given to my demonstration, the following inference might be drawn:

> "It is the capitalist who reaps all the advantage from machinery. The working class, if it suffers only temporarily, never profits by it since, by your own showing, they displace a portion of the national labour without *diminishing* it, it's true, but also without *increasing* it."

I do not pretend, in this slight treatise, to answer every objection; the only end I have in view is to combat a vulgar, widely spread and dangerous prejudice. I want to prove that a new machine only causes the discharge of a certain number of hands, when the remuneration which pays them is abstracted by force.[33] These hands and this remuneration would combine to produce what it was impossible to produce before the invention; whence it follows, that the final result is *a beneficial increase of production by the same amount of labour.*

Who is the gainer by these additional benefits?

First, it is true, the capitalist, the inventor; the first who succeeds in using the machine; and this is the reward of his genius and courage. In this case, as we have just seen, he effects a saving in the expense of production, which in whatever way it may be spent (and it always is spent), employs exactly as many hands as the machine caused to be dismissed.

---

33 It seems Bastiat is referring here to the deadening effect of taxation, stifling innovation and economic activity.

But soon *competition* obliges him to lower his prices in proportion to the saving itself; and then it is no longer the inventor who reaps the benefit of the invention: it is the purchaser of what is produced, the consumer, the public, including the workman; in a word, mankind.

And that which is not seen: that the savings gained by all consumers creates a fund whence wages may be supplied, and which replaces the jobs that the machinery has displaced.

Thus, to recur to the previous example, James Goodman obtains a profit by spending two *francs* in wages. Thanks to his invention, the hand labour costs him only one *franc*. So long as he sells the thing produced at the same price, he employs one workman less in producing this particular thing, and that is what is seen; but there is an additional workman employed by the *franc* which James Goodman has saved. This is that which is not seen.

When, by the natural progress of things, James Goodman is obliged to lower the price of the thing produced by one *franc*, then he no longer realises a saving; then he has no longer a *franc* to dispose of to procure for the national labour a new production. But then another gainer takes his place, and this gainer is mankind. Whoever buys the thing he has produced pays a *franc* less, and necessarily adds this saving to the fund of wages; and this, again, is what is not seen.

Another solution, founded upon facts, has been given of this problem of machinery.

It was said: machinery reduces the expense of production, and lowers the price of the thing produced. The reduction of the profit causes an increase of consumption, which requires an increase of production; and, finally, the introduction of as many workmen, or more, after the invention as were necessary before it. As a proof of this, printing, weaving, etc., are given as examples.

This demonstration is not a scientific one. It would lead us to conclude that if the consumption of the particular item of which we are speaking remains stationary, or nearly so, machinery must displace labour. However, this is not the case.

Suppose that in a certain country all the people wore hats. If, by machinery, the price could be reduced half, it would *not necessarily follow* that the consumption of hats would be doubled.

Would you say that in this case a portion of the national labour had been paralysed? Yes, according to the crude demonstration; but not according to mine.

No; for even if not a single hat more should be purchased by the people, the entire fund of wages would still be secure. That which failed to go to the hat-making trade would be found to have gone elsewhere to the economy supported by all the consumers, and would thence serve to pay for all the labour which the machine had rendered useless, and to excite a new development of all the trades.

And thus it is that things go on. I have known newspapers to cost eighty *francs*, now we pay forty-eight: here is a saving of thirty-two *francs* to the subscribers. It is not certain, or at least necessary, that the thirty-two *francs* should take the direction of the journalist trade; but it is certain, and necessary too, that if they do not take this direction they will take another. One person makes use of them for taking in more newspapers; another, to get better living; another, better clothes; another, better furniture. It is thus that the trades are bound together. They form a vast whole, whose different parts communicate by unseen canals: what is saved by one, profits all. *It is very important for us to understand that savings never take place at the expense of labour and wages.*

9. Credit

In all times, but more especially of late years, attempts have been made to extend wealth by extending credit.

I believe it is no exaggeration to say, that since the revolution of February, the Parisian presses have issued more than 10,000 pamphlets, crying up this solution of the social problem.

The only basis, alas! of this solution, is an optical delusion—if, indeed, an optical delusion can be called a basis at all.

The first thing done is to confuse cash[34] with produce, then paper money with cash; and from these two confusions it is pretended that something real can be made.

It is absolutely necessary in this question to forget money, coin, bills, and the other instruments by means of which productions pass from hand to hand. Our business is with the products themselves, which are the real objects of the loan; for when a farmer borrows fifty *francs* to buy a plough, it is not, in reality, the fifty *francs* which are lent to him, but the plough; and when a merchant borrows 20,000 *francs* to purchase a house, it is not the 20,000 *francs* which he owes, but the house. Money only appears for the sake of facilitating the arrangements between the parties.

Peter may not be disposed freely to lend his plough, but James

---

34 Cash backed by a real asset like gold or silver, as opposed to paper money printed without real assets to give it enduring worth.

may be willing to lend his money. What does William do in this case? He borrows money of James, and with this money he *buys* the plough from Peter.

But, in point of fact, no one borrows money for the sake of the money itself; money is only the medium by which to obtain possession of products. Now, it is impossible in any country to transmit from one person to another more products than that country contains.

Whatever may be the amount of cash and of paper which is in circulation, the whole of the borrowers cannot receive more ploughs, houses, tools, and supplies of raw material, than the lenders altogether can provide; for we must take care not to forget that every borrower supposes a lender, and that what is once borrowed implies a loan.

This granted, what advantage is there in institutions of credit? They facilitate, between borrowers and lenders, the means of finding and dealing with each other; but it is not in their power to cause an instantaneous increase of the things to be borrowed and lent. And yet they *ought* to be able to do so, if the aim of the reformers is to be attained, since they aspire to nothing less than to place ploughs, houses, tools, and provisions in the hands of all those who desire them.

And how do they intend to effect this? By making the State security for the loan.

Let us try and understand the subject, for it contains something which is seen, and also something which is not seen. We must endeavour to look at both.

We will suppose that there is but one plough in the world, and that two farmers apply for it.

Peter is the possessor of the only plough which is to be had in France; John and James wish to borrow it. John, by his honesty, his property, and good reputation, offers security. He inspires confidence; he has credit. James inspires little or no confidence. So, naturally, Peter lends his plough to John.

But now, according to the Socialist plan, the State interferes and says to Peter, "Lend your plough to James, I will be security for its return, and this security will be better than that of John, for he has no one to be responsible for him but himself; and I, although it is true that I have nothing, dispose of the fortune of the tax-payers and it is with their money that, in case of need, I shall pay you the principal and interest."

And so Peter lends his plough to James: this is what is seen.

And the Socialists rub their hands, and say, "See how well our plan has answered. Thanks to the intervention of the State, poor James has a plough. He will no longer be obliged to dig the ground; he is on the road to make a fortune. It is a good thing for him, and an advantage to the nation as a whole."

Indeed, it is no such thing; it is no advantage to the nation, for there is something behind which is not seen.

It is not seen, that the plough is in the hands of James, but only because it is not in those of John.

It is not seen, that if James farms instead of digging, John will be reduced to digging instead of farming.

Consequently, what was considered an increase of loan is nothing but a displacement of loan. Besides, it is not seen that this displacement implies two acts of deep injustice.

It is an injustice to John, who, after having deserved and already obtained credit by his honesty and activity sees himself robbed of it.

It is an injustice to the tax-payers, who are made to pay a debt which is no concern of theirs.

Will anyone say that Government offers the same facilities to John as it does to James?

But as there is only one plough to be had, two cannot be lent.

The argument always maintains that thanks to the intervention of the State, more will be borrowed than there are things to be lent; for the plough represents here the bulk of available capital.

It is true, I have reduced the operation to the most simple expression of it, but if you submit the most complicated Government institutions of credit to the same test, you will be convinced that they can have but one result; that is, to displace credit, not to augment it.

In one country, and in a given time, there is only a certain amount of capital available—and all is invested. By guaranteeing the insolvent, the State may indeed increase the number of borrowers, and thus increase interest rates (always to the disadvantage of the tax-payer), but it has no power to increase the number of lenders or what is available for loan.

There is one conclusion, however, which I would not for the world be suspected of drawing. I say that the law ought not *to favour*, artificially, the power of borrowing. But neither ought it *to restrain* them artificially. If, in our system of mortgage, or in any other, there be obstacles to the diffusion of the application of credit, let them be got rid of; nothing can be better or more just than this.

But this is all which is consistent with liberty, and it is all that any who are worthy of the name of reformers will ask.

10. Algeria

Here are four orators disputing for the platform. First, all the four speak at once; then they speak one after the other. What have they said?

Some very fine things, certainly, about the power and the grandeur of France; about the necessity of sowing, if we would reap; about the brilliant future of our gigantic colony;[35] about the advantage of sending to a distance the surplus of our population, and so on and so forth.

Magnificent pieces of eloquence, and always adorned with this conclusion: "Vote fifty million *francs*, more or less, for making ports and roads in Algeria; for sending emigrants there; for building houses and developing the land. By so doing, you will relieve the French workman, encourage African labour, and give a stimulus to the commerce of Marseilles. It would be profitable every way."

Yes, it is all very true, if you take no account of the fifty million *francs* until the moment when the State begins to spend them; if you only see where they go, and not whence they come; if you look only at the good they are to do when they come out of the tax-gatherer's bag, and not at the harm which has been done, and the good which has been prevented, by putting them into it. Yes, at this limited point of view, all is profit.

---

35 Algeria at this time was a French colony. France, like many European powers, sought colonies to augment its wealth and prestige.

The house which is built in Barbary[36] is that which is seen; the harbour made in Barbary is that which is seen; the work caused in Barbary is what is seen; a few less hands in France is what is seen; a great stir with imports and exports at Marseilles is still that which is seen.

But, besides all this, there is something which is not seen. The fifty millions expended by the State cannot be spent, as they otherwise would have been, by the tax-payers. It is necessary to deduct, from all the good attributed to the public expenditure which has been effected, all the harm caused by the prevention of private expense, unless we say that James Goodman would have done nothing with the money that he had earned, and of which the tax had deprived him. It's an absurd assertion, for if he took the trouble to earn it, it was because he expected the satisfaction of using it.

He would have repaired the palings in his garden, which he cannot now do, and this is that which is not seen. He would have manured his field, which now he cannot do, and this is what is not seen. He would have added another story to his cottage, which he cannot do now, and this is what is not seen. He might have increased the number of his tools, which he cannot do now, and this is what is not seen. He would have been better fed, better clothed, have given a better education to his children, and increased his daughter's marriage portion; this is what is not seen. He would have become a member of the Mutual Assistance Society[37], but now he cannot; this is what is not seen. On one hand, note all the enjoyments of which

---

36 Barbary: North African coastal region, including Algiers, Tunis, Tripoli, Morocco.

37 Before the advent of the welfare state across the Western world, there were many such voluntary societies which people joined to benefit one another through co-operation.

he has been deprived, and the means of action which have been destroyed in his hands; on the other, are the labour of the drainer, the carpenter, the smith, the tailor, the village schoolmaster, which he would have encouraged, and which are now prevented. All this is what is not seen.

Much is hoped from the future prosperity of Algeria; be it so. But the drain which France is being subjected to ought not to be kept hidden. The commerce of Marseilles is pointed out to me; but if this is to be brought about by means of taxation, I shall always show that an equal commerce is destroyed thereby in other parts of the country.

It is said, "There is an emigrant transported into Barbary; this is a relief to the population which remains in the country," I answer, "How can that be, if, in transporting this emigrant to Algiers, you also transport two or three times the capital which would have served to maintain him in France?"

The only object I have in view is to make it evident to the reader that in every public expense, behind the apparent benefit, there is an evil which it is not so easy to discern. As far as in me lies, I would make the reader form a habit of seeing both and taking account of both.

When a public expense is proposed, it ought to be examined in itself, separately from the pretended encouragement of labour which results from it because this encouragement is a delusion. Whatever is done in this way at the public expense, private expense would have done all the same; therefore, the interest of labour is neither here nor there.

It is not the object of this treatise to criticise the intrinsic merit of the public expenditure as applied to Algeria, but I cannot withhold a general observation. It is this: that the prudent presumption is always *unfavourable* to collective expenses by way of tax. Why? For this reason:

First, justice always suffers from it in some degree. Since James Goodman had laboured to gain his wealth, in the hope of receiving a gratification from it, it is to be regretted that the Treasury should interpose through taxation, and take from James Goodman this gratification, to give it upon another.

Certainly, it behoves the Treasury or those who regulate it to give good reasons for this. It has been shown that the State gives a very aggravating reason, when it says, "With this money I shall employ workmen."

James Goodman (as soon as he hears it) will be sure to answer, "That is all very fine, but with this money I might employ them myself!"

Apart from this reason, others present themselves with clarity and the debate between the Treasury and poor James becomes much simplified. If the State says to him, "I take your money to pay the gendarme, who saves you the trouble of providing for your own personal safety; for paving the street which you are passing through every day; for paying the magistrate who causes your property and your liberty to be respected; to maintain the soldier who maintains our frontiers."

James Goodman, unless I am much mistaken, will pay for all this without hesitation.

But if the State were to say to him, "I take your money that I may give you a little prize in case you cultivate your field well; or that I may teach your son something that you have no wish that he should learn; or that the Minister may add another to his score of dishes at dinner; I take it to build a cottage in Algeria, in which case I must take more money every year to keep an emigrant in it, and another hundred *francs* to maintain a soldier to guard this emigrant, and yet more money to maintain a general to guard this soldier," etcetera.

I think I hear poor James exclaim, "This system of law is very much like a system of cheat!"

The State foresees the objection, and what does it do? It jumbles all things together, and brings forward just that provoking reason which ought to have nothing whatever to do with the question. It talks of the effect of these *francs* upon labour; it points to the cook and purveyor of the Minister; it shows an emigrant, a soldier, and a general, living upon the money; it shows, in fact, what is seen.

And if James Goodman has not learned to take into the account what is not seen, James Goodman will be fooled. And this is why I want to do all I can to impress it upon his mind, by repeating it over and over again.

As the public expenses displace labour without increasing employment, a second serious presumption presents itself against them. To displace labour is to displace labourers and to disturb the natural laws which regulate the distribution of the population over the country. If 50,000,000 *francs* are allowed to remain in the possession of the tax-payers since the tax-payers are everywhere, they encourage activity in the 40,000 parishes in France. They act like a natural tie, which keeps every one upon his native soil;

they distribute themselves amongst all imaginable labourers and trades. If the State, by drawing off these 50,000,000 *francs* from the citizens, accumulates them, and expends them on some given point, it attracts to this point a proportional quantity of displaced labour, a corresponding number of labourers, belonging to other parts; a fluctuating population, which is out of its place, and I venture to say dangerous when the fund is exhausted.

Now here is the consequence (and this confirms all I have said): this feverish activity is, as it were, forced into a narrow space; it attracts the attention of all; it is what is seen. The people applaud; they are astonished at the beauty and facility of the plan, and expect to have it continued and extended.

But that which they do not see is that an equal quantity of labour, which would probably be more valuable, has been displaced from over the rest of France.

11. Frugality and Luxury

It is not only in public expenditure that *what is seen* eclipses *what is not seen*. Setting aside what relates to political economy, this phenomenon leads to false reasoning. It causes nations to consider their moral and their material interests as contradictory to each other.

What can be more discouraging or more dismal?

For instance, there is not a father of a family who does not think it his duty to teach his children order, system, the habits of carefulness, of economy, and of moderation in spending money.

There is no religion which does not thunder against pomp and luxury.

This is as it should be; but, on the other hand, how frequently do we hear the following remarks:

> "To hoard money is to bleed the people dry."

> "The luxury of the great provides comforts for the little."

> "Prodigals ruin themselves, but they enrich the State."

> "It is the excesses of the rich which makes bread for the poor."

Here, certainly, is a striking contradiction between the moral and the social idea.

How many eminent people, after having made the assertion, repose in peace! It is a thing I never could understand, for it seems to me that nothing can be more distressing than to discover two opposite tendencies in mankind. What?—mankind comes to degradation at each of the extremes: economy brings people to misery; prodigality plunges them into moral degradation.

Happily, these vulgar maxims exhibit economy and luxury in a false light, taking account only, as they do, of those immediate consequences which *are seen*, and not of the distant ones, which *are not seen*. Let us see if we can clarify this incomplete view of the case.

Mondor[38] and his brother Aristus[39], after dividing the parental inheritance, have each an income of 50,000 *francs*. Mondor practises the fashionable philanthropy. He is what is called a squanderer of money. He renews his furniture several times a year; changes his wardrobe every month. People talk of his ingenious contrivances to bring them sooner to an end: in short, he surpasses the extravagances of Balzac and Alexandre Dumas.[40]

Thus everybody is singing his praises.

> "Tell us about Mondor! Mondor for ever! He is the benefactor of the workman; a blessing to the people. It is true, he revels in dissipation; his carriage splashes the passers-by; his own dignity and that of human nature are lowered a little; but what of that? He does good with his fortune, if not with himself. He causes money to circulate; he always sends the tradespeople away satisfied. Is not money made round that it may roll?"

---

38 Mondor refers to a character on the Parisian boulevards: a type of charming street-hustler.

39 Aristus is a character, a decent and kind man, in a play by Moliere.

40 Honore de Blazac and Alexandre Dumas were French authors renowned for spending money (and for their debts).

Aristus has adopted a very different plan of life. If he is not an egotist he is, at any rate, an individualist, for he considers expense, seeks only moderate and reasonable enjoyments, thinks of his children's prospects. In short, he *economises*.

And what do people say of him?

> "What is the good of a rich fellow like him? He is a skinflint! There is something imposing, perhaps, in the simplicity of his life; and he is humane, too, and benevolent, and generous, but he *calculates*. He does not spend his income; his house is neither brilliant nor bustling. What good does he do to the paper-hangers, the carriage makers, the horse dealers, and the confectioners?"

These opinions, which are fatal to morality, are founded upon what is seen: the expenditure of the prodigal.

But there is another which is not seen: the equal and even superior expenditure of the thrifty.

Matters have been so admirably arranged by the Divine inventor of social order, that in this as in everything else, political economy and morality, far from clashing, agree. The wisdom of Aristus is not only more dignified, but still more *profitable*, than the folly of Mondor. And when I say profitable, I do not mean only profitable to Aristus, or even to society in general, but more profitable to the workmen themselves: to the trade of the time.

To prove it, it is only necessary to turn the mind's eye to those hidden consequences of human actions, which the bodily eye does not see.

Yes, the prodigality of Mondor has visible effects in every point of view. Everybody can see his variety of carriages, the delicate paintings on his ceilings, his rich carpets, the brilliant effects of his house. Everyone knows that his horses run upon the turf. The dinners which he gives at the Hotel de Paris attract the attention of the crowds on the Boulevards; and it is said, "That is a generous man; far from saving his income, he is very likely eating into his capital." That is what is seen.

It is not so easy to see, with regard to the interest of workers, what becomes of the income of Aristus. If we were to trace it carefully, however, we should see that the whole of it, down to the last *franc*, gives work to the labourers, as certainly as the fortune of Mondor.

Only there is this difference: the wanton extravagance of Mondor is doomed to be constantly decreasing, and to come to an end without fail. While the wise expenditure of Aristus will go on increasing from year to year. And if this is the case, then, most assuredly, the public interest will be in unison with morality.

Aristus spends upon himself and his household 20,000 *francs* a year. If that is not sufficient to content him, he does not deserve to be called a wise man. He is touched by the miseries which oppress the poorer classes; he thinks he is bound in conscience to afford them some relief, and therefore he devotes 10,000 *francs* to acts of benevolence. Amongst the merchants, the manufacturers, and the agriculturists, he has friends who are suffering under temporary difficulties; he makes himself acquainted with their situation so he can assist them with prudence and efficiency, and to this work he devotes 10,000 *francs* more. Then he does not forget that he has daughters to portion, and sons for whose prospects it is his duty to provide, and therefore he considers it a duty to invest and put out to interest 10,000 *francs* every year.

The following is a list of his expenses:-

     1. Personal expenses—20,000 *francs*.

     2. Benevolent objects—10,000

     3. Loans or gifts of support—10,000

     4. Invested savings—10,000

Let us examine each of these items, and we shall see that not a single *franc* escapes the national economy.

1. Personal expenses. These, as far as workpeople and tradesmen are concerned, have precisely the same effect as an equal sum spent by Mondor. This is self-evident so we shall say no more about it.

2. Benevolent objects. The 10,000 *francs* devoted to this purpose benefit trade in an equal degree; they reach the butcher, the baker, the tailor, and the carpenter. The only thing is that the bread, the meat, and the clothing are not used by Aristus, but by those whom he has made his substitutes. Now, this simple substitution of one consumer for another in no way affects trade in general. It is all the same whether Aristus spends a *franc* or provides some unfortunate person to spend it instead.

3. Loans or gifts of support. The friend to whom Aristus lends or gives 10,000 *francs* does not receive them to bury them; that would be against the hypothesis. He uses them to pay for goods, or to discharge debts. In

the first case, trade is encouraged. Will any one pretend to say that it gains more by Mondor's purchase of a thoroughbred horse for 10,000 *francs* than by the purchase of 10,000 *francs'* worth of stuffs by Aristus or his friend? For if this sum serves to pay a debt, a third person appears, that is, the creditor, who will certainly employ them upon something in his trade, his household, or his farm. He forms another means of exchange between Aristus and the workmen. The names only are changed, the expense remains, as does the encouragement to trade.

4. Invested savings. There remains now the 10,000 *francs* saved. And it is here, as regards the encouragement to the arts, to trade, labour, and the workmen, that Mondor appears far superior to Aristus, although in a moral point of view Aristus shows himself, in some degree, superior to Mondor.

I can never look at these apparent contradictions between the great laws of nature without a feeling of physical uneasiness which amounts to suffering. Were mankind reduced to the necessity of choosing between two parties, one of whom injures his interest, and the other his conscience, we should have nothing to hope from the future.

Happily, this is not the case; and to see Aristus regain his economical superiority, as well as his moral superiority, it is sufficient to understand this consoling maxim, which is no less true despite its paradoxical appearance: "To save is to spend."

What is Aristus's object in saving 10,000 *francs*? Is it to bury them in his garden? No, certainly; he intends to increase his capital and his income; consequently, this money, instead of being employed upon his own personal gratification, is used for buying land, a house, etcetera, or it is placed in the hands of a merchant or a banker. Follow the progress of this money in any one of these cases, and you will be convinced, that through the medium of vendors or lenders, it is encouraging labour quite as certainly as if Aristus, following the example of his brother, had exchanged it for furniture, jewels, and horses.

For when Aristus buys or leases more land for 10,000 *francs*, he is determined by the consideration that he does not want to spend this money. This is why people speak against him.

But, at the same time, the man who sells the land or receives the rent will want to spend the 10,000 *francs* in some way. So the money is spent in any case, either by Aristus or by others in his stead.

With respect to the working class, to the encouragement of labour, there is only one difference between the conduct of Aristus and that of Mondor. Mondor spends the money himself, and around him, and therefore the effect *is seen*. Aristus, spending it partly through intermediate parties, and at a distance, therefore effect *is not seen*.

But, in fact, those who know how to attribute effects to their proper causes, will perceive that what is not seen is as certain as what is seen. This is proved by the fact that in both cases the money circulates, and does not lie in the iron chest of the wise man, any more than it does in that of the spendthrift. It is, therefore, false to say that economy does actual harm to trade; as described above, it is as equally beneficial as luxury.

But how far superior is it if instead of confining our thoughts to the present moment we let them embrace a longer period!

Ten years pass away. What is become of Mondor and his fortune and his great popularity? Mondor is ruined. Instead of spending thousands of *francs* every year in the community, he is, perhaps, a burden to it. In any case, he is no longer the delight of shopkeepers; he is no longer the patron of the arts and of trade; he is no longer of any use to the workmen, nor are his successors, whom he has brought to want.

At the end of the same ten years Aristus not only continues to throw his income into circulation, but he adds an increasing sum from year to year to his expenses. He enlarges the national capital, that is, the fund which supplies wages, and as it is upon the extent of this fund that the demand for hands depends, he assists in progressively increasing the remuneration of the working class; and if he dies, he leaves children whom he has taught to succeed him in this work of progress and civilization.

In a moral point of view, the superiority of thrift over luxury is indisputable. It is consoling to think that it is so in political economy to everyone who, not confining his views to the immediate effects of phenomena, knows how to extend his investigations to their final effects.

12. He Who Has a Right to Work Has a Right to Profit

"Brothers, Government must organise to provide me work at a set price."

This is the right to work; i.e., elementary socialism of the first degree.

"Brothers, Government must organise to provide me with lucrative work at my own price." This is the right to profit; i.e., refined socialism, or socialism of the second degree.

Both of these concepts live upon such of their effects as *are seen*. They will die by means of those effects which *are not seen*.

That which is *seen* is the labour and the profit excited by the social combination. That which is *not seen* is the labour and the profit to which this same combination would give rise if it were left to the tax-payers.

In 1848, the right to labour for a moment showed two faces. This was sufficient to ruin it in public opinion.

One of these faces was called *National workshops*.[41] The other,

---

41 *National workshops* were a type of work-for-the dole scheme that quickly drained the government budget.

Forty-five centimes.[42] Millions of *francs* went daily from the Rue Rivoli to the national workshops. This was the fair side of the medal.

And this is the reverse. If millions are taken out of a cash-box, they must first have been put into it. This is why the organisers of the right to public labour turn to the tax-payers.

> Now, the peasants responded, "I must pay forty-five centimes; then I must deprive myself of some clothing. I cannot manure my field; I cannot repair my house."

> And the country workmen said, "As our townsman deprives himself of some clothing, there will be less work for the tailor; as he does not improve his field, there will be less work for the drainer; and as he does not repair his house, there will be less work for the carpenter and mason."

It was then proved that two kinds of meal cannot come out of one sack, and that the work furnished by the Government was done at the expense of labour, paid for by the tax-payer. This was the death of the right to labour, which showed itself as much a chimera as an injustice. And yet, the right to profit, which is only an exaggeration of the right to labour, is still alive and flourishing.

Ought not the protectionist to blush at the part he would make society play?

He says to it, "You must give me work, and, more than that, lucrative

---

42 *Forty-five centimes* was the common name for a new tax, implemented by a government with a budget in crisis. This additional tax was deeply unpopular and led to angry protests.

work. I have foolishly fixed upon a trade by which I lose ten per cent. If you impose a tax of twenty *francs* upon my countrymen, and give it to me, I shall be a gainer instead of a loser. Now, profit is my right; you owe it me!"

Now, any society which would listen to this sophist, burden itself with taxes to satisfy him, and not perceive that the loss to which any trade is exposed is no less a loss when others are forced to make up for it,—such a society, I say, would deserve the burden inflicted upon it.

Thus we learn by the numerous subjects which I have treated, that, to be ignorant of political economy is to allow ourselves to be dazzled by the immediate effect of a phenomenon. Acquaintance with political economy is to embrace in thought and in forethought the whole compass of effects.

I might subject a host of other questions to the same test; but I shrink from the monotony of a constantly uniform demonstration, and I conclude by applying to political economy what Chateaubriand[43] says of history:

> "There are," he says, "two consequences in history; an immediate one, which is instantly recognized, and one in the distance, which is not at first perceived. These consequences often contradict each other; the former are the results of our own limited wisdom, the latter, those of that wisdom which endures. The providential event appears after the human event. God rises up behind men. Deny, if you will, the supreme counsel; disown

---

43 Francois-Rene de Chateaubriand (1768-1848) was a writer and political figure. He served briefly as Minister of Foreign Affairs from 1822 to 1824.

its action; dispute about words; designate, by the term, force of circumstances, or reason, what the vulgar call Providence; but look to the end of an accomplished fact, and you will see that it has always produced the contrary of what was expected from it, if it was not established at first upon morality and justice." From Chateaubriand's *Posthumous Memoirs*.

What is *Government?*

I wish someone would offer a prize—not of a hundred *francs*, but of a million, with crowns, medals and ribbons—for a good, simple and intelligible definition of the word "Government."

What an immense service it would confer on society!

The Government! What is it? Where is it? What does it do? What ought it to do? All we know is that it is a mysterious personage; and truly it is the most solicited, the most tormented, the most overwhelmed, the most admired, the most accused, the most invoked, and the most provoked, of any entity in the world.

I have not the pleasure of knowing my reader, but I would stake ten to one, that for six months he has been making Utopias, and if so, that he is looking to Government for the realization of them.

And should the reader happen to be a lady, I have no doubt that she is sincerely desirous of seeing all the evils of suffering humanity remedied, and that she thinks this might easily be done, if Government would only undertake it.

But, alas! that poor unfortunate personage, like Figaro[44], knows not to whom to listen, nor where to turn. The hundred thousand mouths of the press and of the platform cry out all at once:

---

44 Figaro, a character beset with employment and personal difficulties in Mozart's opera *The Marriage of Figaro*.

"Organize labour and workmen."

"Do away with egotism."

"Repress insolence and the tyranny of capital."

"Make experiments upon manure and eggs."

"Cover the country with railways."

"Irrigate the plains."

"Reforest the hills."

"Make model farms."

"Found social workshops."

"Colonize Algeria."

"Feed children."

"Instruct the youth."

"Assist the aged."

"Send the inhabitants of towns into the country."

"Equalize the profits of all trades."

"Lend money without interest to all who wish to borrow."

"Emancipate Italy, Poland, and Hungary."

"Rear and perfect the saddle-horse."

"Encourage the arts, and provide us with musicians and dancers."

"Restrict commerce, and at the same time create a merchant navy."

"Discover truth, and put a grain of reason into our heads. The mission of Government is to enlighten, to develop, to extend, to fortify, to spiritualize, and to sanctify the soul of the people."

"Do have a little patience, people!" says Government in a beseeching tone. "I will do what I can to satisfy you, but for this I must have resources. I have been preparing plans for five or six taxes, which are quite new, and not at all oppressive. You will see how willingly people will pay them."

Then comes a great outcry: "No! indeed! what is the merit of doing a thing with resources? Why, it does not deserve the name of a Government! Don't load us with new taxes; we want you to withdraw the old ones. You ought to suppress:

The salt tax.

The tax on liquors.

The tax on postage.

Custom-house duties.

Patents."

In the midst of this tumult, and now that the country has two or three times changed its Government, for not having satisfied all its demands, I wanted to show that they were contradictory.

But what could I have been thinking about? Could I not keep this unfortunate observation to myself?

I have lost my character for ever! I am looked upon as a man without heart and without feeling; a dry philosopher, an individualist, a plebeian—in a word, an economist of the English or American school.

But, pardon me, sublime writers, who stop at nothing, not even at contradictions. I am wrong, without a doubt, and I would willingly retract. I should be glad enough, you may be sure, if you had really discovered a beneficent and inexhaustible being, calling itself the Government, which has bread for all mouths, work for all hands, capital for all enterprises, credit for all projects, oil for all wounds, balm for all sufferings, advice for all perplexities, solutions for all doubts, truths for all intellects, diversions for all who want them, milk for infancy, and wine for old age—which can provide for all our wants, satisfy all our curiosity, correct all our errors, repair all our faults, and exempt us henceforth from the necessity for foresight, prudence, judgment, sagacity, experience, order, economy, temperance and activity.

What reason could I have for not desiring to see such a discovery made?

Indeed, the more I reflect upon it, the more do I see that nothing could be more convenient than that we should all of us have within our reach an inexhaustible source of wealth and enlightenment—a universal physician, an unlimited treasure, and an infallible counsellor, such as you describe Government to be.

Therefore, I want such a Government pointed out and defined, and that a prize should be offered to the first discoverer of this wonder!

For no one would think of asserting that this precious discovery has yet been made, since up to this time everything presenting itself under the name of the Government is immediately overturned by the people, precisely because it does not fulfil the rather contradictory conditions of the program.

I will venture to say that I fear we are, in this respect, the dupes of one of the strangest illusions which have ever taken possession of the human mind.

Man recoils from trouble and from suffering; and yet he is condemned by nature to the suffering of privation, if he does not take the trouble to work. He has to choose, then, between these two evils.

What means can he adopt to avoid both? There remains now, and there will remain, only one way: *to enjoy the labour of others*. Such a course of conduct prevents the trouble and the satisfaction from preserving their natural proportion, and causes all the trouble to become the lot of one set of persons, and all the satisfaction that of another.

This is the origin of slavery and of plunder, whatever its form may be, whether that of wars, impositions, violence, restrictions, frauds, etcetera. All these are monstrous abuses, but consistent with the selfish thought which has given them birth. Oppression should be detested and resisted, but it can hardly be called absurd.

Slavery is subsiding, thank heaven! And our readiness to defend our property prevents direct and open plunder from being easy.

One thing, however, remains. It is the original inclination which exists in all men to divide the lot of life into two parts, throwing the trouble upon others, and keeping the satisfaction for themselves.

It remains to be shown under what new form this sad tendency is manifesting itself.

The oppressor no longer acts directly and with his own powers upon his victim. No, our conscience has become too sensitive for that. The tyrant and his victim are still present, but there is an intermediate person between them, which is the Government—that is, the Law itself.

What can be better calculated to silence our scruples, and, which is perhaps better appreciated, to overcome all resistance? We all, therefore, put in our claim, under some pretext or other, and apply to Government. We say to it,

> "I am dissatisfied at the proportion between my labour and my enjoyments. I should like, for the sake of restoring the desired equilibrium, to take some of the possessions of others. But this would be dangerous. Could not you facilitate the thing for me? Could you not find me a good place? or check the industry of my competitors? or, perhaps, lend me gratuitously some capital, which you may take from its possessor? Could you not bring up my children at the public expense? Or grant me some prizes? or secure me a pension when I have attained my fiftieth year? By this means I shall gain my end with an easy conscience, for the law will have acted for me, and I shall have all the advantages of plunder, without its risk or its disgrace!"

It is certain, on the one hand, that we are all making some similar request to the Government. And on the other hand, it is proved that Government cannot satisfy one party without adding to the burden of the others. Until I can obtain another definition of the word Government, I feel authorised to give my own. Who knows but it may obtain the prize?

Here it is: Government is the great fiction through which everybody endeavours to live at the expense of everybody else.

For now, as formerly, everyone is, more or less, all for profiting by the labours of others. No one would dare to profess such a sentiment; he even hides it from himself. So what is done? A medium is thought of; Government is applied to, and every class in its turn comes to it, and says, "You, who can take justifiably and honestly, take from the public, and we will share the spoils."

Alas! Government is only too much disposed to follow this diabolical advice, for it is composed of ministers and officials—of men, in short, who, like all other men, desire in their hearts, and always seize every opportunity with eagerness, to increase their wealth and influence.

Government is not slow to perceive the advantages it may derive from the part which is entrusted to it by the public. It is glad to be the judge and the master of the destinies of all; it will take much, for then a large share will remain for itself; it will multiply the number of its agents; it will enlarge the circle of its privileges; it will end by appropriating a ruinous proportion.

But the most remarkable part of it is the astonishing blindness of the public through it all. When successful soldiers used to reduce the vanquished to slavery, they were barbarous, but they were not absurd. Their object, like ours, was to live at other people's expense, and they did not fail to do so.

What are we to think of a people who never seem to suspect that *reciprocal plunder* is no less plunder because it is reciprocal; that it is no less criminal because it is executed legally and with calm order; that it adds nothing to the public good; that it diminishes it, just in proportion to the cost of the expensive medium which we call the Government?

And it is this great chimera which we have placed, for the edification of the people, as a frontispiece to the Constitution. The following is the beginning of the introductory discourse:-

> "France has constituted itself a republic for the purpose of raising all the citizens to an ever-increasing degree of morality, enlightenment, and well-being."

Thus it is France, or *an abstraction*, which is to raise the French, *or realities*, to morality, well-being, etc. Is it not by yielding to this strange delusion that we are led to expect everything from an energy not our own? Is it not giving out that there is, independently of the French, a virtuous, enlightened, and rich being, who can and will bestow upon them its benefits? Is not this supposing, and certainly very gratuitously, that there are between France and the French—between the simple, abridged, and abstract denomination of all the individualities, and these individualities themselves—relations as of father to son, tutor to his pupil, professor to his scholar?

I know it is often said, metaphorically, "The country is a tender mother." But to show the inanity of the constitutional proposition, it is only needed to show that it may be reversed, not only without inconvenience, but even with advantage. Would it be less exact to say?—

"The French have constituted themselves a Republic, to
raise France to an ever-increasing degree of morality,
enlightenment, and well-being."

Now, where is the value of an axiom where the subject and the
attribute may change places without inconvenience? Everybody
understands what is meant by this, "The mother will feed the child."
But it would be ridiculous to say, "The child will feed the mother."

The Americans formed another idea of the relations of the citizens
with the Government when they placed these simple words at the
head of their Constitution:--

"We, the people of the United States, for the purpose of
forming a more perfect union, of establishing justice,
of securing interior tranquillity, of providing for our
common defence, of increasing the general well-being,
and of securing the benefits of liberty to ourselves and
to our posterity, decree," and etcetera.

Here there is no chimerical creation, *no abstraction*, from which
the citizens may demand everything. They expect nothing except
from themselves and their own energy.

If I may be permitted to criticise the first words of our Constitution,
I would remark, that what I complain of is something more than a
mere metaphysical subtlety, as might seem at first sight. I contend
that this *personification* of Government has been, in past times,
and will be hereafter, a fertile source of calamities and revolutions.

There is the public on one side, Government on the other,
considered as two distinct beings. The Government is bound to
bestow upon the public, with the public having the right to claim

from the Government all imaginable human benefits. What will be the consequence?

In fact, Government is not maimed, and cannot be so. It has two hands: one to receive and the other to give; in other words, it has a rough hand and a smooth one. The activity of the second is necessarily subordinate to the activity of the first. Strictly, Government may take and not restore.

 This is evident, and may be explained by the porous and absorbing nature of its administrators, which always retain a part, and sometimes the whole, of what they touch. But the thing that never was seen, and never will be seen or conceived, is, that Government can restore more to the public than it has taken from it. It is therefore ridiculous for us to appear before it in the humble attitude of beggars. It is radically impossible for it to confer a particular benefit upon any one of the individualities which constitute the community, without inflicting a greater injury upon the community as a whole.

Our requisitions, therefore, place it in a dilemma.

If it refuses to grant the requests made to it, it is accused of weakness, ill-will, and incapacity. If it endeavours to grant them, it is obliged to load the people with fresh taxes—to do more harm than good, and to bring upon itself from another quarter the general displeasure.

Thus, the public has two hopes, and Government makes two promises: *many benefits and minimal taxes.* Hopes and promises, which, being contradictory, can never be realised.

Now, is not this the cause of all our revolutions? For, between the Government, which lavishes promises which it is impossible to perform, and the public, which has conceived hopes which can never be realised, two classes of men interpose: the ambitious and the Utopians. It is circumstances which give these their cue. It is enough if these vassals of popularity cry out to the people:

> "The authorities are deceiving you; if we were in their place, we would load you with benefits and exempt you from taxes."

And the people believe, and the people hope, and the people make a revolution!

No sooner are their friends at the head of affairs, than they are called upon to redeem their pledge. The people say:

> "Give us work, bread, assistance, credit, instruction, colonies, and with all this deliver us, as you promised, from the claws of the treasury."

The new Government is no less embarrassed than the former one, for it soon finds that it is easier to promise than to perform. It tries to gain time, for this is necessary for maturing its vast projects. At first, it makes a few timid attempts: on one hand it institutes a little elementary instruction; on the other, it makes a little reduction in the liquor tax. But the contradiction is for ever rising before it: if it would be philanthropic, it must fill the treasury; if it neglects its treasury, it must abstain from being philanthropic.

These two promises are for ever clashing with each other; it cannot be otherwise. To live upon credit, which is the same as exhausting the future, is certainly a present means of reconciling them: an attempt is made to do a little good now, at the expense of a great deal of harm in future.

But such proceedings call forth the spectre of bankruptcy, which puts an end to credit.

What is to be done then? Why, then, the new Government takes a bold step; it unites all its forces in order to maintain itself; it smothers opinion, has recourse to arbitrary measures, ridicules its former maxims, declares that it is impossible to conduct the administration except at the risk of being unpopular; in short, it proclaims itself *governmental.*[45]

And it is here that other candidates for popularity are waiting for it. They exhibit the same illusion, pass by the same way, obtain the same success, and are soon swallowed up in the same gulf.

We had arrived at this point in February.[46] At this time, the illusion which is the subject of this article had made more way than at any former period in the ideas of the people, in connexion with Socialist doctrines. They expected, more firmly than ever, that Government, under a republican form, would open in grand style the source of benefits and close that of taxation. The people said:

> "We have often been deceived, but we will see to it ourselves this time, and take care not to be deceived again!"

What could the Provisional Government do? Alas! just that which always is done in similar circumstances: make promises, and gain time. It did so, of course; and to give its promises more weight, it

---

45 It seems, based on the preceding sentence, that Bastiat uses *governmental* to indicate an intrusive and pervasive form of government.

46 In 1848, revolutions were sweeping across Europe. France, too, was in turmoil for several years. When a new republic was proclaimed, it lasted four years.

announced them publicly thus:

> "Increase of prosperity, diminution of labour, assistance,
> credit, gratuitous instruction, agricultural colonies,
> cultivation of waste land, and, at the same time,
> reduction of the tax on salt, liquor, letters, meat; all this
> shall be granted when the National Assembly meets."

The National Assembly meets, and, as it is impossible to realise two contradictory things, its sad task is to withdraw as gently as possible, one after the other, all the decrees of the Provisional Government.

However, in order somewhat to mitigate the cruelty of the deception, it is found necessary to negotiate a little. Certain engagements are fulfilled, others are in a measure begun, and therefore the new administration is compelled to contrive some new taxes.

Now, I transport myself, in thought, to a period a few months hence, and ask myself, with sorrowful forebodings, what will come to pass when the agents of the new Government go into the country to collect new taxes upon legacies, revenues, and the profits of agricultural traffic? It is to be hoped that my presentiments may not be verified, but I foresee a difficult part for the candidates for popularity to play!

Read the last manifesto of the Montagnards,[47] which they issued on the occasion of the election of the President. It is rather long, but at length it concludes with these words:

> "Government ought to give a great deal to the people,
> and take little from them."

---

47 Montagnards: a democratic socialist party.

It is always the same tactics, or, rather, the same mistake.

"Government is bound to give gratuitous instruction and education to all the citizens."

It is bound to give "A general and appropriate professional education, as much as possible adapted to the wants, the callings, and the capacities of each citizen."

It is bound "To teach every citizen his duty to God, to man, and to himself; to develop his sentiments, his tendencies, and his faculties; to teach him, in short, the scientific part of his labour; to make him understand his own interests, and to give him a knowledge of his rights."

It is bound "To place within the reach of all, literature and the arts, the patrimony of thought, the treasures of the mind, and all those intellectual enjoyments which elevate and strengthen the soul."

It is bound "To give compensation for every accident, from fire, inundation, &c., experienced by a citizen." (The etc., means more than it says.)

It is bound "To attend to the relations of capital with labour, and to become the regulator of credit."

It is bound "To afford important encouragement and efficient protection to agriculture."

It is bound "To purchase railroads, canals, and mines; and, doubtless, to transact affairs with that industrial capacity which characterises it."

It is bound "To encourage useful experiments, to promote and assist them by every means likely to make them successful. As a regulator of credit, it will exercise such extensive influence over industrial and agricultural associations, as shall ensure them success."

Government is bound to do all this, in addition to the services to which it is already pledged; and further, it is always to maintain a menacing attitude towards foreigners; for, according to those who sign the programme:

"Bound together by this holy union, and by the precedents of the French Republic, we carry our wishes and hopes beyond the boundaries which despotism has placed between nations. The rights which we desire for ourselves, we desire for all those who are oppressed by the yoke of tyranny; we desire that our glorious army should still, if necessary, be the army of liberty."

You see that the gentle hand of Government, that good hand which gives and distributes, will be very busy under the government of the Montagnards. You think, perhaps, that it will be the same with the rough hand—that hand which dives into our pockets. Do not deceive yourselves.

The aspirants after popularity would not know their trade, if they had not the art, when they show the gentle hand, to conceal the rough one. Their reign will assuredly be the jubilee of the tax-payers!

"It is superfluities, not necessaries," they say "which ought to be taxed."

Truly, it will be a good time when the Treasury, for the sake of loading us with benefits, will content itself with curtailing our superfluities!

This is not all. The Montagnards intend that:

> "Taxation shall lose its oppressive character, and be only an act of fraternity."

Good heavens! I know it is the fashion to thrust fraternity in everywhere, but I did not imagine it would ever be put into the hands of the tax-gatherer.

To come to the details. Those who sign the programme say:

> "We desire the immediate abolition of those taxes which affect the absolute necessaries of life, as salt, liquors, & etc., & etc."

> "The reform of the tax on landed property, customs, and patents."

> "Gratuitous justice—that is, the simplification of its forms, and reduction of its expenses," (This, no doubt, has reference to postage.)

Thus, the tax on landed property, customs, patents, stamps, salt, liquors, postage, all are included. These gentlemen have found out the secret of giving an excessive activity to the *gentle hand* of Government, while they entirely paralyse its *rough hand*.

Well, I ask the impartial reader, is it not childishness, and more than that, dangerous childishness? Is it not inevitable that we shall have revolution after revolution, if there is a determination never to stop till this contradiction is realised: "To give nothing to Government and to receive much from it?"

If the Montagnards were to come into power, would they not become the victims of the means which they employed to take possession of it?

Citizens! In all times, two political systems have been in existence, and each may be maintained by good reasons. According to one of them, Government ought to do much, but then it ought to take much. According to the other, this twofold activity ought to be little felt. We have to choose between these two systems.

But as regards the third system, which partakes of both the others, and which consists in exacting everything from Government, without giving it anything, it is chimerical, absurd, childish, contradictory, and dangerous. Those who parade it, for the sake of the pleasure of accusing all Governments of weakness, and thus exposing them to your attacks, are only flattering and deceiving you, while they are deceiving themselves.

For ourselves, we consider that Government is and ought to be nothing whatever but *common force organized*, not to be an instrument of oppression and mutual plunder among citizens; but, on the contrary, to secure to everyone his own, and to cause justice and security to reign.

From the Manufacturers of Candles, Wax-lights, Lamps, Candlesticks, Street Lamps, Snuffers, Extinguishers, and of the Producers of Oil, Tallow, Rosin, Alcohol, and, generally, Everything connected with lighting

To Messieurs the Members of the Chamber of Deputies.

Gentlemen,—You are on the right road. You reject abstract theories, and have little consideration for cheapness and plenty. Your chief care is the interest of the producer. You desire to emancipate him from external competition, and reserve the *national market for national industry.*

We are about to offer you an admirable opportunity of applying your—what shall we call it? Your theory? No; nothing is more deceptive than theory; your doctrine? Your system? Your principle? But you dislike doctrines, you abhor systems, and as for principles, you deny that there are any in social economy: we shall say, then, your practice, your practice without theory and without principle.

We are suffering from the intolerable competition of a foreign rival, placed, it would seem, in a condition so far superior to ours for the production of light, that he absolutely *inundates our national market* with it at a price fabulously reduced. The moment he shows himself, our trade leaves us—all consumers apply to him; and a branch of native industry, having countless ramifications, is all at once rendered completely stagnant.

This rival, who is no other than the Sun, wages war to the knife against us, and we suspect that he has been raised up by perfidious Albion (good policy as times go); inasmuch as he displays towards that haughty island a circumspection with which he dispenses in our case.

What we pray for is, that it may please you to pass a law ordering the shutting up of all windows, sky-lights, dormer-windows, outside and inside shutters, curtains, blinds, bull's-eyes; in a word, of all openings, holes, chinks, clefts, and fissures, by or through which the light of the sun has been in use to enter houses, to the prejudice of the meritorious manufactures with which we flatter ourselves we have accommodated our country—a country which, in gratitude, ought not to abandon us now to a strife so unequal.

We trust, Gentlemen, that you will not regard this our request as a satire, or refuse it without at least previously hearing the reasons which we have to urge in its support.

And, first, if you shut up as much as possible all access to natural light, and create a demand for artificial light, which of our French manufactures will not be encouraged by it?

If more tallow is consumed, then there must be more oxen and sheep; and, consequently, we shall behold the multiplication of artificial meadows, meat, wool, hides, and, above all, manure, which is the basis and foundation of all agricultural wealth.

If more oil is consumed, then we shall have an extended cultivation of the poppy, of the olive, and of rape. These rich and exhausting plants will come at the right time to enable us to avail ourselves of the increased fertility which the rearing of additional cattle will impart to our lands.

Our heaths will be covered with resinous trees. Numerous swarms of bees will, on the mountains, gather perfumed treasures, now wasting their fragrance on the desert air, like the flowers from which they emanate.

No branch of agriculture will be without a cheering development.

The same remark applies to navigation. Thousands of vessels will proceed to the whale fishery; and, in a short time, we shall possess a navy capable of maintaining the honour of France, and gratifying the patriotic aspirations of your petitioners, the undersigned candlemakers and others.

But what shall we say of the manufacture of *articles de Paris*? Henceforth you will behold gildings, bronzes, crystals, in candlesticks, in lamps, in lustres, in candelabra, shining forth, in spacious warerooms, compared with which those of the present day can be regarded but as mere shops.

No poor *resinier*[48] from his heights on the seacoast, no coalminer from the depth of his sable gallery, but will rejoice in higher wages and increased prosperity.

Only have the goodness to reflect, Gentlemen, and you will be

---

48 *Resinier*: gatherer of resin, a valuable component for various industries.

convinced that there is, perhaps, no Frenchman, from the wealthy coalmaster to the humblest vender of *Lucifer* matches, whose lot will not be ameliorated by the success of this our petition.

We foresee your objections, Gentlemen, but we know that you can oppose to us none but such as you have picked up from the effete works of the partisans of free trade. We defy you to utter a single word against us which will not instantly rebound against yourselves and your entire policy.

You will tell us that, if we gain by the protection which we seek, the country will lose by it, because the consumer must bear the loss.

We answer:

You have ceased to have any right to invoke the interest of the consumer; for, whenever his interest is found opposed to that of the producer, you sacrifice the former. You have done so for the purpose of *encouraging labour and increasing employment*. For the same reason you should do so again.

You have yourselves obviated this objection. When you are told that the consumer is interested in the free importation of iron, coal, corn, textile fabrics—yes, you reply, but the producer is interested in their exclusion. Well, be it so; if consumers are interested in the free admission of natural light, the producers of artificial light are equally interested in its prohibition.

But, again, you may say that the producer and consumer are identical. If the manufacturer gain by protection, he will make the agriculturist also a gainer; and if agriculture prosper, it will open a vent to manufactures. Very well; if you confer upon us the monopoly of furnishing light during the day first of all, we shall purchase quantities of tallow, coals, oils, resinous substances, wax, alcohol—besides silver, iron, bronze, crystal—to carry on our manufactures; and then we, and those who furnish us with such commodities, having become rich will consume a great deal, and impart prosperity to all the other branches of our national industry.

If you urge that the light of the sun is a gratuitous gift of nature, and that to reject such gifts is to reject wealth itself under pretence of encouraging the means of acquiring it, we would caution you against giving a death-blow to your own policy.

Remember that hitherto you have always repelled foreign products, because they approximate more nearly than home products to the character of gratuitous gifts. To comply with the exactions of other monopolists, you have only *half a motive*; and to repulse us simply because we stand on a stronger vantage-ground than others would be to adopt the equation + x + = -. In other words, it would be to heap *absurdity upon absurdity.*

Nature and human labour co-operate in various proportions (depending on countries and climates) in the production of commodities. The part which nature executes is always gratuitous; it is the part executed by human labour which constitutes value, and is paid for.

If a Lisbon orange sells for half the price of a Paris orange, it is because natural, and consequently gratuitous, heat does for the one, what artificial, and therefore expensive, heat must do for the other.

When an orange comes to us from Portugal, we may conclude that it is furnished in part gratuitously, in part for an onerous consideration; in other words, it comes to us at *half-price* as compared with those of Paris.

Now, it is precisely the *gratuitous half* (pardon the word) which we contend should be excluded.

You say, How can natural labour sustain competition with foreign labour, when the former has all the work to do, and the latter only does one-half, the sun supplying the remainder?

But if this half, being gratuitous, determines you to exclude competition, how should the whole, being gratuitous, induce you to admit competition?

If you were consistent, you would, while excluding as hurtful to native industry what is half gratuitous, exclude *a fortiori* and with double zeal, that which is altogether gratuitous.

Once more, when products such as coal, iron, corn, or textile fabrics, are sent us from abroad, and we can acquire them with less labour than if we made them ourselves, the difference is a free gift conferred upon us. The gift is more or less considerable in proportion as the difference is more or less great. It amounts to a quarter, a half, or three-quarters of the value of the product, when the foreigner only asks us for three-fourths, a half, or a quarter of the price we should otherwise pay. It is as perfect and complete as it can be, when the donor (like the sun in furnishing us with light) asks us for nothing.

The question, and we ask it formally, is this, *Do you desire for our country the benefit of gratuitous consumption, or the pretended advantages of onerous production?*

Make your choice, but be logical; for as long as you exclude as you do, coal, iron, com, foreign fabrics, in proportion as their price approximates to zero, what inconsistency would it be to admit the light of the sun, the price of which is already at *zero* during the entire day!

FURTHER READING

Ammous, S. (2023). *Principles of Economics.* The Saif House.

Bastiat, C. F. (1850/2007). *The Law.* Auburn: Ludwig von Mises Institute.

Bylund, P.L. (2022). *How to think about the Economy.* Auburn: Mises Institute.

Fenwick, P. (2022). *The Fortunate: ten great writers highlight how we created free and affluent societies*. Redland Bay: Connor Court.

Hannan, D. (2013). *Inventing Freedom.* New York: Harper Collins.

Hayek, F. A. (1944/2007). *The Road to Serfdom.* London: University of Chicago Press.

Hulsmann, J. G. (2008/2012). *The Ethics of Money Production.* Skyler J. Collins.

Mises, L. v. (1927/2010). *Liberalism.* Auburn: Ludwig von Mises Institute.

Ridley, M. (2011). *The Rational Optimist.* New York: Harper Collins.

Rothbard, M.N. (1982/2002). *The Ethics of Liberty.* New York: New York University Press.

www.ingramcontent.com/pod-product-compliance
Lightning Source LLC
Chambersburg PA
CBHW061259220326
41599CB00028B/5709